I WILL WALK WITH YOU

Following Jesus to the Side
of Those Who Suffer

GREG FISH

WESTBOW
PRESS®
A DIVISION OF THOMAS NELSON
& ZONDERVAN

Scripture quotations marked (NLT) are taken from the Holy Bible, New Living Translation, copyright © 1996, 2004, 2007 by Tyndale House Foundation. Used by permission of Tyndale House Publishers, Inc., Carol Stream, Illinois 60188. All rights reserved.

WestBow Press books may be ordered through booksellers or by contacting:

WestBow Press
A Division of Thomas Nelson & Zondervan
1663 Liberty Drive
Bloomington, IN 47403
www.westbowpress.com
1 (866) 928-1240

ISBN: 978-1-9736-3174-3 (sc)
ISBN: 978-1-9736-3176-7 (hc)
ISBN: 978-1-9736-3175-0 (e)

Library of Congress Control Number: 2018907217

Print information available on the last page.

WestBow Press rev. date: 07/12/2018

In memory of Barbara,
my precious angel.

I'm glad I had the privilege of walking with you.

Acknowledgements

I am grateful to my friend, former pastor, and mentor, Chet Martin, for helping me make this book far better than it would have otherwise been. Your grace and effort in providing edits and suggestions has been a blessing for which I am appreciative.

I am grateful to all of the congregations I have served as pastor for your contributions to my life and ministry. I am particularly grateful to the congregation of Hope Church in Rushville, Illinois, who stood beside me through one of my life's greatest challenges. Your friendship, support and encouragement has allowed me to thrive.

I am grateful to my friends and family who have encouraged me to tell my story. I honor my sister, Stephanie Bates, for her words of affirmation. I am so proud of my daughter, Jackie White, who has helped me process so much of my journey in the light of God's beauty and hope. Jackie, you bring so much sunshine into my world.

I am so grateful that God has brought just the right person into my life to walk with me through this next leg of my journey. Lisa, I will walk with you with joy and thanksgiving! I am so appreciative that you are inspiring me to be the man God has made me to be. Your encouragement makes me better.

I gratefully acknowledge and honor the contributions of my parents, Richard and Florence Fish, whose words of faith and encouragement have accompanied me even long after their earthly lives ended. My late grandparents, Cleo Scott, and Glenn and Ina Fish also have been blessings to my story.

All praise and glory and honor to my Lord, Jesus Christ, who holds all things together, and has held me together through all things.

First Things:
Sit Here With Me For A While

Day after day, time moving in infinite slow motion, I sat by the bedside of my wife Barbara in that cold, gray, intensive care room, the monotony broken only by a visit or a note.

One note came from a friend who sent me a poem from one of my favorites, James Whitcomb Riley. It inspired me to put a few of my own thoughts that day into Rileyesque form.

I wrote the following for those who wanted to console me, but had no words to say.

Sit Here With Me For A While

Sit here with me for a while
Your nearness is enough
'Sides, th' words just come out crooked
The road, it is so rough

The pleasure of your presence
Your echo of my sighs
Far outweighs th' shiny things
Some exchequer supplies

Let our laughter sound through tears
Don't be afraid t' smile
'Cause these days are far too heavy
And I might be here a while

So sit here with me freely
Fearing not the still
For it reads clear that you love me
And assures you always will.

——⟁——

When one of the realities of your life is a spouse who suffers, there are plenty of people who love to give advice (sometimes, the advice is quite good… and then there are those other times…). There are plenty of doctors with plenty of theories. There are plenty of diets and plenty of lines of thinking nutritionally. There are plenty of folk remedies. And in keeping with that, there are plenty of sermons, plenty of speakers, and plenty of books on any range of topics relating to suffering and struggle.

And then there is the matter of help for those who walk beside the one who suffers. Let's just say there is not much out there. It's time for some encouragement, helpful thinking, and spiritual direction for those who tend to the bedsides and pathways of the hurting.

Over the years, many people, including my own father, expressed admiration that I was able to do what I did for a wife who suffered with the near-lifelong debilitating illness of rheumatoid arthritis. I humbly received those kind words realizing that I was only doing what needed to be done to make it from day to day. These lessons have been learned over years of life-schooling. I've often joked with nurses that I've earned my honorary medical degree. I've learned to administer medical devices and position hospital beds better than some hospital staffers. I can change a bed while someone's in it. I'm also told I'm quite good at placing bed pans. Don't get too excited, though; this is not a service I readily offer to the general public.

I've also learned through much refining (in a very 2 Timothy chapter 2 sort of way), that I am able to love someone other than myself in such a way that no debilitation or need can quench my desire to serve them. That doesn't mean it's easy to do so, it just means I finally get why constant repeated hammering can often produce something quite refined and beautiful from silver.

I can whine with the best of them. I've learned what it means to battle worry. I've even discovered that fear is not my enemy, but that it doesn't have to be my master either. Fear can be a good thing if it keeps you from sticking your hand in the rattlesnake pit. But, fear doesn't have to keep you from making right decisions and moving forward into scary places. After all, as a believer in Christ, I know the one who has authority over the most scary stuff of all, and He's been a friend and companion on this journey.

That's the Jesus part of my story. I have learned that if we set out to follow Jesus, we all eventually find ourselves in the role of coming along beside someone who is suffering or struggling. There are those tricky and sneaky parts of Scripture that lurk there waiting between all the sweet passages. Just as we're strolling along through the Bible, suddenly the words jump out and eat our delusions of a life of riches and roses for dinner. It's those pesky parts, like 1 John 3:16 or 1 Peter 2:21, that remind us that we are called to make great sacrifices for each other and for the work Christ has given us to do… and that means laying down our lives willingly for the sake of others.

So what do we do once we've come to grip with the fact that by following Jesus, I've found myself at the side of someone who struggles. What do I do now?

There's the matter of what we say. If you've ever fumbled and juggled words while speaking to someone who just lost a loved one, I have some thoughts for you that I hope will be of value to you each time you enter that kind of situation.

My inspiration on this topic has been multiplied many times over in my role as a pastor as well as a husband. It's very easy for those of us who follow Christ to cling to fatigued ways of dealing with sufferers without being sure how to truly love them. I'm convinced that most of us do care about others. However, we have not had the training on how to show this love. This can lead us to avoid the hurting at all costs, and in doing so, we avoid the very ones Jesus calls us to.

So how do we learn to love well? For the believer in Christ, it's just what we do. It's the road we travel, it's the banner we wave. If we truly intend to follow Christ, then we will quickly find that He will lead us to the side of someone who is suffering. We most assuredly will find ourselves in the very place we might have otherwise avoided for fear of how to respond or react.

Maybe I can help you out a little. Sit here with me for a while, and let me help you feel better about walking beside someone who hurts.

—⟊⟊—

This book is divided into four main sections. First I'll tell you my story, and share some very personal lessons learned.

Next, we'll look introspectively and consider what needs to happen in us to make us ready to walk beside others. The best way to deal with our own uglies, if you will, is to look them in the face and call them by name. We can't fight an enemy we don't know. A look inside ourselves will be a good starting point for looking to the needs of others.

The third section will look outside ourselves as we prepare for how to respond to those who hurt or suffer. This will be, by no means, a complete treatise on all manner of suffering and struggle. Rather than taking a text book approach, I will introduce you to a few lines of encouragement that I hope will prepare you for what you will face when you lock step with the hurting.

Finally, I will give you the keys to the mint; that's my light-hearted way of describing the essential tools that will bring great riches into our relationships. We have a weird view of prosperity in this country. We think it's about money. True prosperity is a richness and fullness of life, a wonderful joy that accompanies us on our journey. That's the mint, and I've got a few keys to share that will open the door to dealing with some of the tougher situations we'll face.

Each chapter will end with a few devotional or group study questions to help you as you weigh what I have said. I'm not presenting edicts to you, but rather, information that I hope will inspire greater thoughts and powerful conversation within your faith groups and at home. I pray that these words will be a blessing to you and create room for growth, joy and wisdom in your life.

Here is what I've found it means to follow Jesus to the side of those who suffer, and to thrive doing so as we offer to walk beside them for a while.

MY STORY

Let me tell you my story. This section will take an intimate look at the events that defined what I know today about what it means to walk with someone who hurts. This is the story of my wife Barbara and the brave life she lived. It's my journey beside her as she struggled with illness, and eventually succumbed. This is the story of how God taught me to walk beside someone who is hurting.

One

BROKEN AND
BEAUTIFUL THINGS

My journey of understanding how to walk with one who suffers began in the summer of '89.

My mother was dying of cancer. It had progressed and spread far beyond the reach of medical intervention. I clearly remember sweating heavily in that tight, hot room stuffed full of family members as the surgeon told us that mom's cancer was a worst-case scenario, and that they would not be able to save her. Our first question was, I'm sure, the most typical.

"How long does she have?"

It's a desperate kind of question that we know has no answer, but seems to be the fitting thing to ask in the moment.

"There's no way to know," he replied frankly. "Maybe a year. Maybe two."

Turns out he was wrong on both counts. But then, how could any education prepare a physician to cipher all the variables and give a definitive answer? It's like the weatherman predicting snow. He knows all the signs, he knows all the conditions, but the result can only be known when it happens. If it happens.

One quiet Sunday night I decided to visit mom in her hospital room to have "the talk." You know what I mean, right? It's that big conversation that deals with all the heavy stuff that we don't want to say. It's the kind of conversation that will certainly make up for the dearth of communication to come in whatever the years ahead hold. It's where you relive joyous moments and steel each other for the storm ahead.

As I sat by her side, bracing myself for the difficult words ahead, my plans were laid to ruin by the arrival of her friend, Dorothy. Don't get me wrong, Dorothy was a hoot. It's just that I didn't want her there interrupting an important mother-son conversation.

Mom and Dorothy were friends from church and co-conspirators in any number of mischievous adventures. At least as mischievous as a church organist and Christian youth leader could be. Mom's resume may have seemed saintly on the surface, but she was a saint with a snicker. And Dorothy knew how to instigate her share of trouble. She was one of those people who you could tease incessantly, and know that she would always be ready to throw it back to you. She was also willing to wear any nickname I could label her with and chortle in response, "God'll getcha for that one someday."

So there we are in the hospital room. The three of us. As the evening progressed, Dorothy turned the conversation to my nonexistent love life. She became determined to set me up, and she knew just the person. She had a neighbor girl who said she was looking for a good guy in a sea of not-so-good ones.

Dorothy set us up. It was a total disaster.

Later, sitting on the front porch of Dorothy's house, along with her daughter Eunice, who was my age, we laughed about what a bad idea the whole arranged date was.

It was at that moment that the match-maker bug bit Eunice. Actually, I think that bug had bored its way into her skull long before. She perked up and said, "I know the one! Barbara Baker!"

My heart stopped. OK, so maybe it didn't really stop but it sure seemed like everything froze in time for just a few seconds. The entire chemical universe of my body did some sort of twirling dance with itself – the type of dance that results in the inevitable smile and an incredible wow.

Back in our junior high years, Eunice had brought a friend with her to Vacation Bible School. I remembered this friend well – Barbara Baker – the girl that I was quite certain was the most beautiful thing I'd ever seen. Her smile was astonishing and her eyes sparkled magically. Even though Barbara was a little older than me, she was always very friendly and outgoing where other kids might have ignored me. I was smitten, but I was also painfully unable to make my affections known. So, in the secret of my room, I scribbled in my journal that one day Barbara Baker and I would be married.

I found that journal years later, and out of total embarrassment threw it in the trash.

So there I sat on that porch with Dorothy and Eunice and the prospect of now dating the girl I once said would be my wife. They told me that her life had taken some bad turns, and that she had a few health issues, but that she was doing well and had a beautiful young daughter named Jackie.

In the days ahead I was overwhelmed when the beautiful Barbara Baker accepted my invite to the blind date at Dorothy and Eunice's house. Barbara would later tell me that she was impressed that I showed up at the date fully prepared with the pizza and a bag of ice for the drinks. She seemed a bit disappointed when I had to admit I was just following orders from Dorothy.

We met for pizza, played cards, and were friends from the very first moment. But Greg is a painfully shy guy. I needed some reassurances, and so a ruse was concocted. At one point in the evening, I would dismiss myself for a bathroom break. While away, Eunice would find out what Barbara thought of me, then give me a signal when I arrived back in the room. A nod meant go for it, a shaking head would call me off.

As I walked in the room, there was Eunice nodding her heading up and down emphatically with an embarrassingly massive smile on her face. Very tactful, Eunice, thank you. But it gave me the courage to press on.

It was years later that I finally confessed the ruse to Barbara. She laughed at me and told me that Eunice never asked her a thing about me. It was all a big giant lie! It was a lie that blessed my life beyond words.

After that night, Barbara and I were practically inseparable. Now let me qualify what I'm about to tell you by saying I would never recommend this to anyone else, but it worked for us.

Barbara and I began dating on August 4. Her daughter Jackie had also captured my heart. Realizing that Jackie needed a dad at home, and also understanding that my mom wouldn't live much longer, Barbara and I became engaged on September 9. To this day I wish I'd come up with an exciting way to propose; it was more like a business decision! I didn't get on my knees, I didn't plan a memorable event. It was a meeting of hearts that happened during a conversation about our future. We decided to get married, and we wanted to do so quickly. We planned to be married on December 29 so that mom could be there.

Mom died near Thanksgiving.

My sister and I were still home preparing a few dishes to bring to the family gathering. Dad called from the hospital. His voice was full of agony. Mom was in the hospital for severe headaches and had been talking to the doctor when tears began to run down her face. She looked at dad and said, "I didn't know it would…" and she was gone. Well, actually she had a massive stroke, but I'm convinced that even though her body lived on for a few additional days, she left us at that moment. So amidst the screams of code blue, dad called with the news.

As a devastated young 24-year-old man, I wondered how I could move forward. But then, how could I not move forward with Barbara and Jackie now the center of my universe? So after a little more than a month of dating and an engagement of not quite four months, we began our journey together. We got married on a late December Friday evening with fog as thick as the proverbial pea soup.

From the early days on, Barbara often warned of the ravages that her rheumatoid arthritis would have on her body. We discussed the horrific ramifications of both the disease and the medications she took. She told me that the medicines she took would both save her life, and threaten it with nasty side effects. We would hold hands and walk side by side dreaming about what was ahead, daring not to fear the uncertain.

I noticed from early on that she grew tired easily. I quickly learned that everything she did was hard to do. I saw her get up and go to work on days when most people would have stayed in bed. She attended nursing school while recovering from hip replacement surgery, and by the time we met and were wed, she was one semester away from graduating. She became a Registered Nurse, and then became aware that her body wasn't quite as forgiving as long nights working a nursing home floor demanded. But she continued to work. Hard.

Barbara did more with her broken body than many of us do with well bodies.

A New Way of Thinking

I wish that I could tell you that I was intuitive to all of her needs, and that I was always kind and considerate of the things that were beyond her ability to control. But there were times when our marriage balanced precariously on a head of a pin and there were days when we both wanted to give up and just get away from each other.

Romans 12:2 reminds us to dare to let our minds be transformed. Renewed. By allowing Christ's presence in us to make us more effective in our role of walking beside others, we are leaving behind the model of the world that encourages us to pursue self-gratification at any turn.

Loving others effectively - giving them what they need most of all - is a process of a transformation of mind. It's not what comes natural. It's a holiness thing that is mindful and needful of the presence of Jesus.

So, before we can go further and learn how to walk beside others, we must first settle in for the renewal-of-mind process that readies us for the task at hand.

Courtship Vs. Marriage

In my years of serving as a pastor, I've counseled many young couples preparing to get married. I've never had a couple sit in my office and say, "If we can't work things out, we'll just get a divorce." Nor have I heard, "I just can't take his or her attitude any longer." However, I have had plenty of couples struggling at the edge of a marriage in crisis say those things. What moves us from blind idealism to exhausted hopelessness?

When Barbara and I were dating, I had no idea of how her disease would one day ravage her. I was sure of myself and my ability to handle anything that would come. There's nothing wrong with confidence or optimism. Frankly, had my response been anything less, Barbara would never have married me and the pastor would never have consented to officiate.

If you are at the beginning point of walking with someone who suffers or struggles, there are no tools I can give you to make your journey glorious or painless. I do, however, offer the following thoughts for you to give serious consideration as you start:

Don't stop at the end of the on-ramp.

Picture this: an already busy interstate road at peak traffic time. Travelers in a hurry to get home or get to work. Every lane packed with cars, and precious little room to merge between them. Next, see yourself on the on-ramp, preparing to enter the mayhem. You accelerate, knowing that your first priority is to match the speed of the oncoming traffic. Suddenly, you hear a scream. As your neck is turned observing a possible entry point, the person sitting next to you has just realized that the car in front of you on the on-ramp has ground to a halt. They are paralyzed with fear.

Yes, this really happened to me. My only option was to dash over to the shoulder, passing the fearful motorist, and then do my best from there to get off the side and into traffic. As I passed the parked car on the wrong side, they honked, as if indignant that I had to maneuver to miss them.

Driving can be challenging work at times, but you can't do it if you are sitting still. Just think about that one for a moment.

Fear can paralyze us, and cause us to shirk away from oncoming challenges. It can also create anger or resentment.

Remember this, though. The driver who stopped at the end of the on-ramp was fearful of the traffic on the interstate, but should also have exercised a healthy fear of the traffic coming up from behind.

Don't let fear paralyze you. Yes, life is dangerous, tough, wild and unruly at times. Keep moving. Keep going.

Don't fight the shot.

Like many others, when I was a young boy I hated getting shots. It's not that I've become fond of them now, but I once was paralyzed by the prospect of the sharp poke.

I remember the day at the doctor's office that I thought I was going to get off easy without a medicinal invasion when the doctor announced that I indeed would be nicked by the needle. My hands gripped the arms of the chair, frozen in horror. I remember my dad pulling on me from one side, and the doctor from the other. There was a nice fat spot there below me that would serve well as the introduction point for the cure. Once they were able to pry me loose and get me properly bent over, pants down around my ankles, I found that despite the humiliation of it all, the shot itself bothered me very little. In fact, I have lived a full life since having successfully survived the occasion. I even got candy afterwards despite the fact that I wasn't the most cooperative of patients. The Dum Dum lasted a lot longer than the syringe.

There will be plenty of unpleasant zones ahead as you walk this path. Choose to live this life, not to fight it. When the painful moments hit, remind yourself that survival requires moving forward. Best of all, as we walk with Christ, we have a great hope that there is so much more to gain than there is to lose.

Pick Your Mentors Well

There will be plenty of nay-sayers and detractors along the way.

As a pastor, I've been told by church people and denominational leaders that I should just give up. I struggled for years feeling like a failure because I believed the lie that Barbara's health struggles were detrimental to ministry. In fact, it was our very submission to this journey that led to some of the most powerful ministry opportunities. Barbara's life as a pastor's wife impacted many people. I had the opportunity to demonstrate fidelity and integrity by walking with her through many challenges. If I had listened to those who told us to give up, I wonder how many people might have been untouched by a message of hope and redemption.

I wouldn't suggest seeking to surround yourself with sycophants and yes-men. However, when you find a prayer warrior that can deliver a word of encouragement or a challenging admonition that breathes full of the breath of the Spirit, make them your mentor.

You need mentors in this journey. Pick them well.

Read Romans 12:2, then spend some time in James 2 as well.

1. Greg wrote, "Barbara did more with her broken body than many of us do with well bodies." How does that challenge you to keep moving? Who have you known that has accomplished amazing

things despite personal challenges? What things are you let impair your journey?

2. What did Greg mean when he talked about courtship vs. marriage? What are some of the ways we can stay encouraged as we transition from the early days to the difficult days of learning?

3. How does grace encourage us to act rather than sit on the sidelines? What are some of the inevitable actions we will take when we follow Jesus?

4. Has there ever been a time when you were paralyzed by fear? How did you get back on your feet? What things inspired you to act?

5. Think of people who have truly ministered Jesus into your life. What were their qualities? How did they encourage you or challenge you?

A blessing prayer for you:

May God's grace and mercy inspire you to acts of grace of mercy towards others. May your starting points be blessed with courage and hope, and may the difficult days abound with courage and hope as well. May God's love empower you as you serve others.

Two

LIFE AFTER DEATH

Marriage is a delicate, stony path. It's not about happily-ever-after or a prince and princess riding off into the sunset. It's difficult and grueling and painful. It's also a conundrum because at the same exact time, it can be sweet and rewarding and glorious. Marriage is about holiness. It's about two stubborn, selfish personalities coming together and learning how to get along with each other. This union purposefully calls us to submit to each other so that we in turn become better citizens in the community around us.

In 2006, after almost 17 years of marriage, Barbara and I seemed to be on the marital low road without many returns to the top. Barbara was becoming increasingly dependent upon me due to the ongoing ravages of rheumatoid arthritis (RA) and the requisite medicines. The arguments became more frequent. I resented having to help her do so many of her routine tasks, and she resented that I had to help her. I hated the fact that I had to do all the laundry and she hated the way I did the laundry. I hated the fact that I had to do all the cooking and she wasn't terribly fond of my culinary choices.

Doing ministry work together was also becoming grueling, and we were at odds more than at evens. Neither one of us were happy with the direction things were going. She became increasingly confined to the house and resented it when I was able to get out and do even the most routine tasks of ministry. Leaving to go to my office in the church became a point of contention because it meant that I was getting out of the house while she could not. The problem was only exacerbated by the increasing, tormenting neck pains that continued to flare. By November an MRI was ordered to see if the problem could be pinpointed. And thus began the whirlwind.

We lived in the shadow of Chicago at that time, and one of the nation's leading neurosurgeons, a man we'd never met, was asked to review Barbara's case and offer an opinion. Normally it would have taken months to get an appointment with him, but he insisted she show up at his office immediately. She was quickly placed into a neck brace, and we learned that the damages of the RA had caused her spine to impinge the spinal cord to the point where it was about to snap.

She was rushed in for surgery, and then, due to poor bone condition, a second surgery.

RA is caused by a body's immune system gone crazy. Oversimplification, sure, but that captures the big picture. The medicines given to treat it lower your ability to fight off infections, and hospitals can be a dangerous place for someone with a compromised immune system as they are a breeding ground for infections.

In the hospital for these emergency surgeries, Barbara developed pneumonia. Then came other infections. She was put into an induced coma and lay on life support for over a month. Along the way she died twice and was resuscitated. The doctors called us into a conference to prepare us for the inevitable. Barbara would not survive. Even if she did, she would be confined to a bed and likely in a halo for the rest of her life. A halo is a bracing device used to hold the head perfectly still at all times.

Now there's some news that will punch you in the gut.

I remember reading about King Hezekiah.

> About that time Hezekiah became deathly ill, and the prophet Isaiah son of Amoz went to visit him. He gave the king this message: "This is what the lord says: 'Set your affairs in order, for you are going to die. You will not recover from this illness.'" When Hezekiah heard this, he turned his face to the wall and prayed to the lord, "Remember, O lord, how I have always been faithful to

you and have served you single-mindedly, always doing what pleases you." Then he broke down and wept bitterly. Then this message came to Isaiah from the lord: "Go back to Hezekiah and tell him, 'This is what the lord, the God of your ancestor David, says: I have heard your prayer and seen your tears. I will add fifteen years to your life… (Isaiah 38:1-5, NLT)

I didn't see this so much as a specific promise but rather a prominent reminder of God's grace and mercy. I made these words my own and chose to believe them as I pled for Barbara. My confidence in God remained strong, and I sensed that I must continue to serve my congregation on Sundays as a demonstration of God's power. After all, if I couldn't live out what I say I believe, how could I expect anyone else to do so? Through those days I only missed one Sunday. I'm not saying this is the right approach for everyone, but it was the way the Spirit led me.

My strength seemed to be increasingly swallowed up in weakness and frailty. Week after week, Barbara's health deteriorated and there was little hope to be found in the words of doctors. Then came Fayth.

Words of Fayth

Fayth was a five-year-old in my congregation who prayed for Barbara every day. She didn't have a shy bone in her body. So I asked her if she would come forward and pray for Barbara one Sunday. I will never forget the prayer as she stood there confidently by the altar rail. There wasn't a dry eye in the room as her squeaky little-girl voice rang out with confidence:

"Dear Jesus, please don't let Miss Barbara die."

That day, a remarkable turnaround began.

Not long after that, Barbara was brought out of her coma and began to acknowledge us. At first it was with silly, goofy smiles. Eventually her brain began to clear, and all remaining vestiges of life support were removed. Even more remarkably, she began to move her hands and arms.

Barbara was always an avid crafter and was well known for making beautiful baby blankets. The day came in the hospital when Barbara asked me to bring her some yarn and a hook so she could see if she could still crochet. Knowing that she didn't need anything discouraging to block her progress, I hesitantly brought in the items, afraid that the result would be devastating. But I'd forgotten about the great healing work that God had begun. Her first attempts to crochet the yarn were loosely formed and not at all up to her standards. But within days her broken hands began to form the start of a blanket. She began to create beautiful afghans to give away.

In all, Barbara was in hospitals and rehab units for eight months.

Making It To The Wedding and the Marriage

There was one other challenge. In May, our daughter Jackie was to get married in Lexington, Kentucky. This was, under the best of conditions, about a five-and-a-half-hour drive away. Between issues of frail health and hospital check-out regulations, there was no way she should have been able to attend the wedding. But then, God provided the way. Barbara, sick and delicate, saw Jackie and Peter get married and we survived the very taxing journey.

The wedding story was brought together as intricately as one of Barbara's afghans. Many strands found miraculous union, things happened that weren't supposed to happen, and impossibilities became possible as God intervened on our behalf. This would be a great story alone if it were just about the wedding. But there's so much more. It's also about the marriage.

The crucible of those days forged Barbara and I into more useful instruments for ministry. Barbara received healing for damaged emotions and found the ability to give forgiveness for a deep wound from her past. I learned that I was strong enough to do things I never thought I could do while becoming skilled at navigating medical systems. The story of those days wasn't just about our daughter's wedding. It was also about saving our own marriage. We fell in love again and became wiser and more empowered than ever before to serve well as a pastoral couple.

Neither one of us ever found much peace regarding my laundry skills. However, my cooking improved. I would occasionally become her sous-chef, although it required much patience from both of us.

It broke her heart that all of the household chores fell onto my shoulders. It didn't help that I was a below-average housekeeper lacking in time or patience for the job of keeping a house in order. It was a profound blessing that over the years we were able to have several wonderful people help us with the job of housekeeping.

I knew that I had been given what I came to know as "bonus years" with my wife. She died, and then came back to me. There was a long period of time where we could have no conversation, and now there was renewed life in our words to each other. It was in these hospital days that I gained a new name for Barbara. As my broken heart wondered if she would survive, I asked the nurses to take good care of my precious angel. From that day forward, that's who she was to me. My precious angel. I think it also became a special, endearing connection with many of those who served her in those days; it seems they were moved hearing me speak of her in that way.

All of this doesn't mean life got easy. In fact, it was more difficult than ever before. From that point forward, Barbara was confined to a wheel chair and her care needs were far greater. But thankfully, she survived what she should not have survived, and we enjoyed the richest, most meaningful years of married life and ministry work.

Towards the end of Barbara's stay in a rehab facility, I was able to check her out on special occasions. By "check her out," I'm talking like a book and not a look!

I remember the first day I was able to pick her up on a Sunday morning. It was her first time back in church after months of respirators, IV's, surgeries and therapies. We arrived at the sanctuary before everyone else. As I pushed her down the aisle, I realized she was sobbing. I then felt obliged to join her in tears. No words can properly express the sanctity and beauty of a moment like that. Out of death, back to life, and in the beautiful house of worship where we'd invested so much of our lives.

We Want A Marriage Like Yours

It is such a blessing to officiate a wedding, and each wedding adds a unique and precious page to my memory book. In the year after Barbara returned home, I performed a marriage for a sweet couple who were combining families. It was the second marriage for both, and they were especially aware of the things that can go wrong.

We spent several Sundays, after church, enjoying meals together and encouraging each other. Nothing could have prepared Barbara and I for the question that came up during one of those meetings.

We were enjoying our favorite local Mexican restaurant when things took a decidedly serious turn. "We were wondering if you would mentor us in our marriage," they asked, "because we want…"

Nothing could adequately have prepared us for the weight of the last half of this inquiry…

"…We want a marriage just like yours."

Barbara and I exchanged a quick, flummoxed glance. They thought we had an ideal marriage? Wow!

We agreed to do this for them and were truly honored. Later, though, we privately wondered if they truly knew what they were asking for. Really? You want a marriage like ours? Do you have any idea of what things are like behind the scenes at the Fish household?

A little more time and wisdom has brought this request into a new light for me. God had given Barbara and I such a wonderful gift in our relationship that it had shown all over us. Why wouldn't others want what we had? God had given us a richness and maturity in our ability to meld two lives together that it sent out an important message of hope to others who wanted the same. It's not that we had a perfect union. It's not that we didn't still struggle. But we had been able to allow God to work through our humanness and frailty in a way that brought a certain sanctification to our lives.

I had become meticulously careful to meet all of Barbara's needs because she was no longer able to do so many things for herself. And she demonstrated a peace, resilience and even cheerfulness through adversity that others found to be winsome. Indeed, why wouldn't others want that? I can't brag on what I was able to do for Barbara, but I can boast about what God did through me. Barbara didn't want to walk the road she had to walk, but she was willing to do so if God could be glorified through her response to it.

> Therefore I (Paul), a prisoner for serving the Lord, beg you to lead a life worthy of your calling, for you have been called by God. Always be humble and gentle. Be patient with each other, making allowance for each other's faults because of your love. Make every effort to keep yourselves united in the Spirit, binding yourselves together with peace. Ephesians 4:1-3 (NLT)

Lessons From A Prisoner

I resonate with Paul's preface in this statement more than I ever have at any other point of my life. He begins by letting us know that he's about to give us a key to the mint - access to something of great, great value. Knowing that it would be hard to accomplish this thing of great value, he begins by reminding us that he had to endure some pretty rough stuff in order to gain this wisdom. We don't really want to discuss what conditions were like for Paul in prison, but having suffered there for the Name of Jesus, he has earned some hard-gained information about what it truly means to live a life worth living.

I haven't endured anything even close to what Paul endured. But I've been to some low places and done some acts of servanthood that I never thought I would have to do (or for that matter, acts that none of us ever want to have to do). Those refining moments are learning moments.

The fact that you've come this far with me probably indicates that you're ready and willing to hear what it takes to walk beside those who hurt and suffer, and to do so in a manner that speaks the Name of Jesus to others who observe what is happening. I remind you of these things:

1. Always be humble and gentle.

It's possible to be humble without being gentle. I assure you that when you have to do the most humbling of acts for another person, there are moments when you want to respond to them in a less than humble manner. You want to scream, you want to cry, you want to vomit. But don't. Instead, take a deep breath and be gentle. Remember that the person you are helping would rather not be in the position they are in. If you demonstrate to them how much you are suffering in order to serve them, uh, humbly, you are not serving their deepest need. Gentleness allows us to smile and reassure in appropriate ways as we do the thing our friend or loved one needs us most to do.

Years ago I was stranded at the roadside with a blown tire, and discovered that the stowed temporary replacement tire was not usable. The person I was able to contact happened to be my boss, the general manager of the radio station I worked at back then. I remember him humbly coming to my aid, giving my family use of his car to get them safely home, and then, without reservation, helping me resolve the tire issue. He did so without complaint or hesitation. It was one of those moments when my respect for him grew infinitely. Moreover, he allowed me to not feel humiliated by the event through his humility and gentleness. He also taught me, in that moment, how to better serve others when they were most vulnerable.

2. Be patient with each other.

Make every allowance for the need of the person you're serving. Barbara once scolded me because I seemed impatient when people wanted to talk to me as their pastor. I would look at my watch, or clearly not be paying attention. Being patient is hard, but not being patient is rude, insulting and can even cost you the respect of others.

I had to learn that when someone wanted to talk with me, that was the only job I had at that moment. No matter how many things I felt pressing on me, I needed to stop and be attentive in the Name of Jesus! Have I perfected this? I suspect not. But I have gotten much better. Getting better is the result of learning to love more. It ties in so directly with this next point that Paul actually made them one and the same in Ephesians:

3. Lovingly allow others to have faults.

Most conflict arises because we do not allow others to have faults, but we are insistent upon receiving grace for our own downfalls. Being patient with the one we serve means being able to look beyond the fact that, just like me, they have faults too. Sometimes those faults cannot be helped. Sometimes those faults develop because of the great weight we bear. Sometimes faults occur just simply because the pressure is so great, none of us could stand up straight underneath the strain.

You or I do not want to have to rely on someone else to perform the most menial of tasks for us. Likewise, we don't want to be in the position where we cannot move forward unless someone else intercedes. Following Jesus to the side of someone who is hurting and has need means that we must also make allowances for the fact that they are going through something that nobody, myself included, wants to go through.

4. Remember it's God who holds all things together.

As we make every effort to allow God's Holy Spirit free reign in us, we find the end result is, consistently, peace. It's what the songwriter meant when he wrote, "It is well with my soul." It doesn't mean we've arrived at a place where all is perfect and fun and easy. But it does mean that whatever mess remains at the end of the day, we can have peace knowing that God has allowed us to be a part of bringing a sense of peace to others. He is the very one who holds us together when we're falling apart.

In the first chapter of Colossians we're reminded that Christ holds all things together. He brings unity to a universe in disarray. He brings a joyful sound where the singers aren't in perfect harmony with each other.

Maybe that's what you need to know more than anything else I can tell you in this book. You need to know that whatever road you find you're on, Jesus is the means to keeping it all together. If you must walk beside a spouse that is ill and cannot fend for their self, or if you must change a tire for some poor soul at the side of the road, it's the arms of Jesus wrapped around you that gives you the freedom to feel peace and give a reassuring smile to the one you're helping.

—m—

Read Ephesians 4:1-3, taking special note of the terms he uses to describe how we should treat others.

1. If you are married, what is your story? Think of the crisis points and how you've dealt with them. Was there a "Jesus factor" involved in how you moved through your difficulties? If you are not married, perhaps you can examine a close relationship that has been strained at times.

2. Why do you think the story of King Hezekiah (Isaiah 38:1-5) was so inspirational? What can we learn about how God deals with us in times of great emotional distress?

3. Can you think of a time that you helped someone, and had to do something unpleasant in order to make their load lighter? Perhaps you had to do very tiring work for them? What did your

attitude display to that other person? Do you see the importance of gentleness as we do humble work for others? Can you think of a time that someone agreed to help you, but you were embarrassed to see that they really didn't want to be rendering aid?

4. Do you agree that we expect much better behavior from others than we ourselves are willing to demonstrate? Is this something you need to lay down at an altar before God and seek transformation?

5. Take a moment to simply bask in the knowledge that God loves you dearly. He's quite fond of you. As you bow your head, allow yourself to visualize and feel Christ's real presence there with you. Know His comfort now.

A blessing prayer for you:

May the love of the Father flow freely from all that you do. May you have a sense of the wealth of love and mercy you have, and may it overflow into all that you do and say.

Three

THE HARDEST
CHAPTER TO WRITE

You might not have realized that RA can be deadly. You might have thought of it in terms of aching hands or knees as one grows older. When I tell people that my wife died of RA, they sometimes look at me quizzically as if I'd just told them she'd died of a splinter.

The disease took its hold on Barbara when she was just 19. Imagine living the majority of your life - for her it was over 30 years - with an insidiously painful disease.

As for me, even though I always knew we probably wouldn't grow old together, I always thought there would be one more year. After all, she was tough; she fought hard and came back in the face of great odds.

Barbara was one of the strongest people I've ever known. She had continued her nursing school education while also receiving a hip replacement. She trudged ahead and became an RN. Though you could tell she walked with a different gate, most people didn't realize that she was in near constant pain. Even in her later years when confined to a wheel chair, her marvelous smile and sparkling eyes belied the inner pain of not being able to do the things she longed to do.

Over time I saw the disease rob Barbara of the meaningful things most of us take for granted. There came the point when she could no longer work. She had to give up driving. She wanted to walk. She wanted to see (cataracts and glaucoma are the residuals of the medicines she had to take – and they were beginning to taunt her). She wanted to walk beside me and hold my hand again, rather than have me walk behind her and push. I wanted that, too.

Since the beginning of our relationship, Barbara warned me what her RA would eventually do. We had years of conversation. But, I don't think you really believe it until you see it. And it is devastating.

Precious Angel

During the time that Barbara spent 8 months in the hospital – the beginning of our "bonus years" – I found myself calling her by a new name. She was my precious angel. The nurses really seemed to like to hear me call her that, so I did so regularly, every time she was in the hospital. I'd say, "Take care of my precious angel for me!" It was a name that seemed to be etched on my deepest soul. Every time I was reminded just how fragile Barbara was, I remembered just how precious she was to me.

One of the greatest pains Barbara endured in her final years had nothing to do with the physical. In fact, we had both felt a peace that God HAD healed her, and that the remainder of our struggle together was something we would willingly submit to God so that others might know more about Him. The greatest pain was not being able to hold her grandchildren. I never took for granted that when I held those warm bodies close to me, I had a privilege that she was only able to enjoy vicariously through me. Even now the pain I saw in her eyes brings me to tears.

Jackie, our daughter, and her family were home with us for Christmas of 2014. It was also the celebration of our 25th anniversary. The grandkids, ages 1 and 2, were such a special treat. One evening something completely unexpected happened as our grandson was being put to bed. He gave me a big hug and kiss. Then to our amazement, as I held him close to Barbara, he wouldn't let her go. He held on to her gently but firmly. With me supporting his weight, he laid his little head on her shoulder and began to breathe heavily. Barbara began to cry. I began to cry. Jackie began to cry. My arms were beginning to cramp holding him like that, but I determined that they would have to fall off of my body before I'd end this precious moment. Barbara got to hold that little boy that night, and it is an event etched in my memory as in granite.

Barbara had been having trouble breathing for most of that year, and heading into 2015, we had an appointment to find out what was going on. She was sleeping a lot and had little to no energy. Everything she did required her to make up her mind that she would do it, and then to move onward. One night, through tears, I asked, "You're not doing well, are you?" "No. No, I'm not," was the reply. Then there was silence as we both cried ourselves to sleep.

Barbara and I would often talk about the earlier hospitalization when she had died. I told her about how devastated I was at the prospect of losing her. She would rub my back and share my pain in much the same way I shared her pain. "I'm so sorry," she would say. It wasn't her fault, of course, but she would console me with those words so that I could see into her heart. I love the way, for no reason, she would at times cheerfully burst into an "I love you!"

"I love you, too! What brought that on?" I'd ask.

"I was just thinking about how wonderful a husband you are."

Telling you that feels a bit self-serving, but I wanted you to know what a beautiful soul this woman had. Even in the middle of her own pain, she had time for mine.

Our nights had become an endless parade of her waking me to assist her in getting to the bathroom. It seemed unfathomable that one person could have to pee so much! Every night, throughout the night, up and down, in and out of her chair.

In mid-January, in the small hours of the early morning, the ending began. She couldn't transfer herself back into her chair, and her left side was numb. We both became agitated realizing that clearly she was having a stroke. I rushed her to the hospital.

Pray That No One Dies Tonight

The stroke led to her bowels shutting down. The doctors were mystified as to the cause, and she was in intense pain. One day a couple from the church stopped by and prayed with her. To the surprise of us all, she joined the prayer with the voice of an angel. It was one of the most beautiful prayers I'd ever heard her pray.

Later that day, our favorite nurse stopped by and Barbara asked how she could pray for her. "Pray that no one dies on my watch tonight!" the nurse replied.

Around 3:30 that morning, after a restless night, Barbara went into cardiac arrest. I was severely sleep deprived at that point, and I remember thinking that somehow I was responsible because I had slipped off to sleep for a few moments. In all my years of caring for her, I had never been through such a horrible experience; it was as close to having a complete breakdown that I'd ever been.

This hospital apparently didn't use the term "code blue." Perhaps it had become too disturbing for patients to hear over the intercom. Instead, the stoic voice summoned a "cart" to her room number. You don't realize how many medical professionals are on the job in the middle of the night until such a thing occurs. While I was being comforted in the hallway, they managed to bring her back. They allowed me to come into the room before they took her to the intensive care unit. She was wild-eyed and confused, but responded that she knew who I was.

In the aftermath of the resuscitation, we discovered that the RA had progressively damaged her body leading to the stroke, the bowel shutdown, and the cardiac arrest. An MRI scan of her torso revealed that her lungs had shrunken to a frighteningly small size, explaining the difficulty breathing. The tour of her inner workings revealed one problem after another. It was quite horrific to view.

Barbara seemed quite clear-minded at that point, and could respond to us despite the respirator tubes in her mouth. On more than one occasion it would be one of those thousand-tear-time moments for me as I realized she was actually mouthing the words of the worship music I played for her. Chris Tomlin's beautiful song, "Jesus Loves Me," was one she seemed to especially love. It would end up being the last song she heard on this earth.

If I ever feel like complaining about my situation, I'm going to remember her on that ventilator, mouthing the words of worship songs despite the tubes going down her throat.

In the midst of a life now full of parades of doctor teams and beeping IV meters, a precious gift arrived via video text. Our one-year-old granddaughter said "Mimi" (their name for grandma) for the first time. As I showed Barbara the video Jackie had sent, her face beamed and she appeared to be helping the baby speak… "Mi… mi…".

A steady flow of wonderful friends from our church came by to look after me. Barbara always lit up for visitors. There was one dear lady who had been inspired by Barbara to look at her aging body's hardships in a new light. She wanted one last moment with the inspirational friend she'd only know for a short time. They brought her back to the room in her wheelchair, and she stood up at the bedside. As if on cue, Barbara's dim eyes sparkled, and her radiant smile beamed out around the tubing. Sometimes goodbyes are precious.

Then things changed. Barbara began to disconnect from the world. Her worship became more intense, and her desire for anything of this life seemed to evaporate.

One day I asked her, "Are you ready to go home and see Jesus?" and she nodded an emphatic yes.

The next day, as our family stood around her, touching her lovingly as she struggled for breath. It broke my heart to see her struggle, and feeling the presence of the Holy Spirit on me, I laid hands on her and told her to be well in the Name of Jesus.

About five years earlier, a precious, dear saint of the church I pastored had a seizure during morning worship and died. There was no pulse, and other signs of death were present. Feeling the Holy Spirit on me, I laid hands on her and said, "Pat, be well in the Name of Jesus". Immediately Pat opened her eyes and was well. I have never forgotten the feeling of being an observer; clearly I was just a willing vessel at that point. That was exactly how I felt as I prayed over Barbara.

I knew in my heart that she would either rise up out of that bed and dance, or that she would, well, rise up out of the bed and dance in Heaven, in a perfect body. I found myself telling her to run. "Don't stop. Run, girl, run." Those were my words, but they weren't mine.

My sister later told me it was if I was escorting her to the gates of Heaven. You know, that's just how it felt. Where Barbara had been struggling monstrously, the Spirit-led prayers quickly escorted her home. It was one of the most amazing things I've witnessed in my life.

In '06, during the 8 month hospital stay, Barbara died twice (and nearly a third time). She came back telling about seeing a very beautiful woman walking towards her. When she asked who the woman was, she was told, "It's you."

Barbara stepped into the body of that beautiful woman she had long been anticipating on February 26, 2015. She was 51 years old. On earth, she was beautiful. Today, she is beautifully perfect. Running, dancing, worshipping, maybe even driving cars. I wouldn't even be surprised if she gets regular visitation with the grandbabies, though that's not orthodox theology – just a musing from the heart of a child of a Father who loves to give good gifts.

The hardest thing I ever had to do for Barbara was to walk her home that day. I think I must've placed her hand into Jesus' hand and said, "Here's my precious angel."

"I know," He would have responded. "And I love her more than you can imagine."

When The Strong Are Weak

In Christian marriage we are reminded that we are made one flesh together. That is so true. How does one go on after their flesh has been torn apart?

Day by day, deep breaths, holy pauses with the Savior: that's how.

Many friends, a great church community, and the hope of glory ahead: that's how.

These things propel me forward. The hurt is considerable, but every morning I wake up with renewed purpose and determination that God has not set me on this journey as some sort of joke; I have a hurting community to serve and they need to know that it is well.

You need to know this: you can live, you can thrive, you can enjoy the full of life even in the midst of great sorrow. Our great hope is not lost, and God still loves you deeply. Though our bodies, our fragile containers, were not made to last, we have a certain hope of so much more.

As you follow Christ to the side of those who are hurting, you will hurt with them. It's an interesting paradox that in being strong for others, we in turn must face our own weakness. There is nothing at all wrong with that. We might easily remind each other that it's through our own weakness that we are compelled to lean on the strength of God. That's true, but I also see something different at work.

Footprints In The Sand?

I understand that the poem "Footprints In the Sand," has been a meaningful piece of contemporary poetry for many. It has been displayed on the walls of many households of believers.

My father, in his struggle with cancer, referenced how meaningful it had been to him.

In the poem, a man looks back over his life, represented by a beach. He sees two sets of footprints, his and God's. However, at the times of his greatest struggle he only sees one set of footprints in the sand. He asks God why he was abandoned during those times. God replies that he was not abandoned, but rather, those were the places where God carried him.

I don't mean to at all detract from something that has been so meaningful to so many, but it just hasn't worked that way for me. I look back and see the two sets of footprints even in the struggle. I ask God, "Why didn't I get the same deal others apparently got? Why didn't you carry me?" His response in my soul comes gently and with great peace, but as a Father that has to teach a son a life-affirming lesson. "Greg, I didn't carry you. Those time of struggle - those were when I taught you how to walk by my strength."

> I have called you back from the ends of the earth,
> saying, 'You are my servant.'
> For I have chosen you
> and will not throw you away.
> Don't be afraid, for I am with you.
> Don't be discouraged, for I am your God.
> I will strengthen you and help you.
> I will hold you up with my victorious right hand.
> Isaiah 41:9-10 (NLT)

Being a servant of God means serving others. I realize now that by learning to serve Barbara and her needs, I've learned to serve others a bit better. I still find it difficult not to open containers for others because I did it so long for her. I still find that my super-strength, my Jason Bourne type skill, is to be able to walk in a room and quickly survey the hazards. When I see someone struggle to walk, I instinctively want to offer them aid. As we give ourselves to others in coming along beside them in their dark hours, we learn how to walk in the strength of the Lord. This is such a needful thing in this life. Never feel as though your life is being wasted or thrown away; your life is being refined for special purposes that are ordained by the Most High! (Read 2 Timothy 2:20-21.)

Don't be afraid: God is with you. Discouragement is the tool of the enemy. Discouragement may even come from the lips of those claiming to represent God, but don't be deceived. Don't be discouraged because God is teaching you how to walk by His strength. He may not carry you, but he will hold you up with His strong, victorious hand.

I remember when dad taught me how to ride a bike. He spent a lot of time running along beside me at first. Eventually, though, he backed off as I figured out that I could operate that contraption on my own. When I fell and cut my knee (this was back in the day before hyper-vigilance prevailed and knee pads became standard fare), dad picked me up, cleaned my wound, and put me back on the bike to ride. I carried a scar for years that reminded me that I could overcome challenges and learn to do good things.

Be strong, be courageous. Know that God is Your God, and He is strong and a good teacher. You will hurt. You will struggle too. You will learn. Then, in time, you will be strong enough to offer this God-gift to others you serve.

I titled this, "The Hardest Chapter To Write," and it was. It was hard because of all the emotions that telling this story still brings to the forefront in me. It was hard because it represented the most difficult lessons learned in life. It was hard because I wanted to go beyond telling you a story packed with high emotional content, and hopefully communicate that the hard things are good things. They are places where we truly learn to walk. It's not easy, but it's needful. It's not simple, but you will be well.

Ponder the words of Isaiah 41:9-10 and imagine hearing God himself gently saying those words afresh to you.

1. What is your most life-defining moment so far in life? How can God help you use that story to help others?

2. Who has most exemplified to you what it means to walk with God through a difficult time? How was their example different than those you've known who have gone through difficulty without a relationship with God?

3. Find the statements you consider most encouraging from the Isaiah passage. Why do they encourage you? Are they hard things to remember when the hurting is greatest? Consider committing these verses to memory so that you will have them near when you most need them.

4. Has your experience in hardship been that God has carried you, or that He has taught you to walk? Why do you suppose we experience this sort of strengthening in different ways?

A blessing prayer for you:

May the Lord give you peace beyond anything you might reasonably expect. May your days be strengthened with the knowledge of our Savior. May you take courage and live fully in the glow of the Father's love surrounding you now.

A LOOK INSIDE

At some point you will find yourself coming along beside someone else who hurts. Let me walk beside you for a while as we take a look into our hearts. Let's think about some things that will help you as you struggle to give care to someone who is struggling.

Four

THE EYES HAVE IT

Mrs. Richardson was one of the most popular teachers at my junior high school.

I was blessed to have her for several classes, but also as my homeroom teacher one memorable year. A year, that is, with one gaping hole of time in the middle.

Mrs. Richardson mysteriously disappeared from the scene for what seemed like an eternity. The substitutes would not offer not a clue as to her whereabouts, leaving perplexed students to speculate.

I vividly remember the day of her return to the classroom. To our surprise, she came striding into our midst with her trademark, gigantic smile, wildly waving her hand in the air. Almost immediately, you could hear echoes of, "Wow!" throughout the room as we were stunned to see how slender she had become in her absence.

One student whispered, "She must've taken time off to lose weight!" Another quickly scolded, "No, you dummy, she had cancer."

Had. It was the necessary word to fill the triumphant moment with its deserved hope. Had cancer... not has... but, had.

Years later my heart would break to learn that Mrs. Richardson had a return of the insidious disease, and this time, she had succumbed to its fury. I don't tell you this to make you sad over the loss of a valuable educator. Rather, I want to share with you the legacy that Mrs. Richardson continues to have in my life. She made the kind of lifelong difference in me that every teacher hopes they'll eventually make in one of their students. I just wish I could tell her today.

In my younger years (and perhaps, into my adulthood more than I'd like to admit), I struggled against negativism, whining, moaning and groaning. I had a very low sense of self-worth - one that at times would leave my mother in tears. I've come a long way in my battle thanks to the grace of Christ. But I owe a special debt of gratitude to one shining moment when a favorite teacher set me onto the road to better thinking.

My negative attitude blazed like an inferno during my junior high years. One morning I decided to seek comfort from Mrs. Richardson, sure that she would have a sympathetic shoulder to cry on. Much to my surprise she began pounding her fist on her desk as she defiantly uttered words that have stayed with me throughout my life. She said, "If you don't stop with this negative attitude, your life is going to be...," picture now her fist pounding the table in rhythm with these words, "...one bad thing after another."

She didn't really say, "bad thing." She actually used a much stronger invective. It may have been the very shock value of the language she chose that woke me up. I can't tell you that I immediately perfected the ability to only think on wonderful things, but the gauntlet was laid before me, and I accepted its wisdom. Even today when I struggle with hope perception, I hear Mrs. Richardson, pounding her desk, reminding me that this is not how I want my life defined.

Whatever organization you find yourself a part of, you have experienced your share of moaners and groaners. You would think that churches, with our great reason for hope and great joy, would be free of them. Oh, I'm sure you're not one of them - our negative words are always meant to be helpful, right? - but you know exactly the attitudes of which I speak.

Often, when confronted with someone who is struggling in an oppressive situation that causes them to stay self-focused, I recommend seeking out someone to serve. Perhaps start as simply as anonymously paying someone's tab at a restaurant. Or, send encouraging notes. The act of focusing outward has great value in addressing our own bent towards negativity. But let's take that a step further now. Let's go the Philippians 4:8 route.

Philippians 4:8? "Fix your thoughts on what is true, and honorable, and right, and pure, and lovely, and admirable. Think about things that are excellent and worthy of praise."

These are much more than light, airy words that lift our spirits and edify us on Sunday mornings. These are important principles that change our lives, and give our community the hope it deserves. There must be a purposeful desire to set our eyes on something better than our own traumas as we do helpful, healing work in the lives of others. As the pursuit of Jesus takes us to the side of the hurting, this is the place where we most need to stay fixed on things that are true, honorable and right. It's good to make pureness and loveliness the subject of our intense gaze. If it's excellent? Admirable? Worthy of praise? Gaze on it! Otherwise, we will be consumed by the agonizing work of sharing the weight of someone's struggle.

Aching Eyes, Glaring Hope

There were times during Barbara's many medical adventures that I found myself having to do something I never wanted to have to do. There were times that, in the interest of monitoring a bad situation, I had to set my eyes on wounds or sores. It was in the interest of her health that I had to steel my stomach for the hard stuff of healthcare. These processes gave me an infinite appreciation for healthcare professionals and the often thankless work they have to do.

When we care, we look on. We oversee. We contemplate, we evaluate, and we act.

Perhaps you have been led to the side of someone who struggles or suffers with chemical addictions or the scars of abuse. Perhaps your attention has been focused on someone who is bitter or depressed. Every level of care has it's ugly side. This is not the place for our own penchant for negativity to be engaged. Even if you consider yourself a positively energized person, the day to day struggle in the face of hurt can wear down the best of us.

Our eyes will grow tired of looking at pain, at seeing the wounds, at overseeing the care of the helpless. Mercy blazes from the very one who led us to this place. Fix your eyes there. Meditate on His Word day and night. Let nothing tear your aching eyes away from His glaring hope.

1. Recite prayers over the one who hurts.

Bless them repeatedly. Pray for good things. Will the very hope of God into their lives by your words. Be bold, be brave and pray endlessly. If you run out of prayers, borrow the words of others. Pray the Psalms - this is an ancient tradition we've forsaken today. Pray the dark Psalms, then revel in the hope that comes after the struggle. Pray the exuberant Psalms and allow their light to inhabit even the grayest rooms.

2. Tell stories.

Tell your best stories of hope and grace. Borrow the stories of others. Tell appropriate jokes. Don't ever be afraid of laughter, but use it wisely. Take you and the one in your care on journeys of the mind. Don't rely on television to put you into a stupor and help you pass time - be generous with your conversation.

3. Have backup.

Have your own team of encouragers. I utilize this often in my role as pastor. Ministry can be a brutal, humiliating, depressive job at times. I don't know how I would have survived this long without strategic encouragers in my life cheering me on, praying for me, and offering me frequent words of hope.

Ten Thousand Lightning Bolts

It was a combination of fear and thrill, an emotional sweet and sour, as I watched the phenomenal displays of might and majesty flashing overhead.

The night sky was filled with lightning, muffled by clouds appearing orange in the suddenly bright firmament. It was a mind blowing display of electrical bolts firing from east to west, continuously, in multiple spots at the same time. I'm not sure how long the display lasted, but it seemed unending. It was if it were the end of the world. And I felt fine.

I later learned that the lightning was from a storm some 90 miles away.

Under the right conditions, lightning can be seen for quite a distance. I don't recall ever witnessing a spectacle like that before.

Never forget that the things you do, the words you say, the choices you make, are ten thousand lightning bolts. You may feel like no one notices. Or you might think that the decisions you make are only your business. But none of us live in a vacuum. We are on display, and the things we do matter. Self-serving motives or generous actions all make a difference in the world around us.

In the moments of greatest despair, when you most wonder if you're really making a difference, remember that making an impact that will last means you might have to forsake momentary assurances.

If you ever watch a science fiction show involving time travel, there is always a warning given to those who travel into the past. Remember that everything you do will change the future. Even though we know that time travel is the stuff of story-tellers, we shouldn't miss the truth that saturates the fiction. As we live out our lives, our decisions matter. No matter how much we may long for them to go unnoticed, it's nearly impossible to keep them from having an impact on others at some level.

We are sending out ten thousand lightning bolts. They will be seen. They will have an impact on others.

I'm convinced that this is precisely why Jesus calls us to walk with the hurting. We need to understand how important we are, despite our feelings of inadequacy or insignificance. The best remedy for these feelings is loving others better.

Occasionally you'll hear someone in the church long for that old time religion. In fact, there's even a song about that. "Give me that old time religion," it begins. There is even the astounding claim that the singer wants the same thing Paul and Silas had. Jail time for believers? Really? Are you sure you are prepared for that? True old time religion (I use the word "religion" with full recognition of the negative connotation it has taken on in many minds today) found the first believers selling all their possessions, living together communally, and selflessly fulfilling the needs of others. We're a long way from that, baby! Perhaps what we're truly longing for, and should rightly be the object of our affection, is to be a part of a community that seeks to make sure that no one has to go it alone through the valley of hurt, struggle or depression.

I say all this still bristling a bit at my own inadequacy. But when I discover that one of my lightning bolts has made a positive impact on someone, my joy overflows. Perhaps the most temperate response to this is to give more focus to the intentional dumb things we do and less credence to the unintentional mistakes we fall into. We're not going to get this absolutely right, but we can reach for something better.

You are ten thousand lightning bolts. You are capable of good things because the one who made you put that capacity in you. Let us sharpen each other in our communities of faith so that we can get better at others-focused ministries. Let us delve deeply into our walk with Christ so that we can look a little more like Him each day. Let us shine with His glory so that others will thrill when it lights up their dark night sky.

—◆—

Read Philippians 4:8 several times and consider how these words impact your plans for the next few days..

1. Think about a hero in your life who told you something you may not have wanted to hear, but set you on a course towards positive change. If you're using a group setting for these questions, share your stories. Focus particularly on how that person helped you to be better at serving the needs of others.

2. Take a moment to actually write out a brief prayer of blessing for someone who you know that is hurting. Make it a point to pray this prayer regularly for the person over the course of the next week. Whether you do this in secret or sharing it with this one you care about, make note of the subtle changes in your heart. How can those positive moves encourage you and reinforce you for the service that lies ahead?

3. Who is your backup? Make sure your prayer and support people are varied in personality and background. You will most certainly need someone who is more spiritually mature than you are. Also think of someone who is a good encourager. Find a support person who is steeped in the Word of God. Regularly seek these out for prayer, accountability and inspiration. Focus too on finding

someone who has been down a similar road and seems to have survived it well. These folks will be invaluable as your backup network.

4. Has someone ever told you that something you said really made a positive difference for them? That felt pretty good, didn't it?! Imagine, then, the force of regularly spoken words of encouragement. How can you be more intentional about speaking helpful, affirming, encouraging things into the lives of others? What things might stop you? Does Philippians 4:8 help you to better focus on how to encourage others?

5. I like to regularly pray, "Lord, let Your glory rise." I remember first praying this as I watched steam rise off of a pond in the early morning hours. It was as if God's very presence was making itself known to me. Visualize a moment like this as you pray for the glory of God to be known in your community, in your life, and especially to the one you come along beside. Make the prayer personal. Pray, "Lord, let Your glory rise in me."

A blessing prayer for you:

May the presence of the Father be known to you, and shown through you. May your soul be so encouraged that words of hope naturally flow from you into the lives of others.

Five

I'M SORRY I SAID A BAD WORD IN CHURCH

It was that time of year when graduation pictures abound on Facebook. I'm often startled by celebrations for those that are locked in my mind as little children, but have mysteriously grown to adult proportions. Occasionally an older adult reminds me that I have outgrown their memory of me as a child!

Once again I found myself taken aback as I scrolled through my newsfeed. I happened upon a set of pictures that left me stunned. Just look at that... who would have thought that the passage of 12 years could take that sweet little six year old boy I remember so fondly and place him on the verge of manhood?

There he was. Tall and handsome in full celebration mode with cap and tassel on his head, and gown flailing open to let in the cool air. I imagined him relieved to be out of that stuffy gymnasium after going through the time honored ritual of receiving a diploma while nearly being suffocated to death.

But the happy-faced graduate surrounded by family wasn't the young boy I remembered.

My little friend was just a scrawny fellow who attended a church I pastored. He was surrounded by older siblings and cousins who loved nothing more than to tease and torment the youngest of the brood. One

Sunday they were being especially hard on my little buddy, to the point he could take it no more. Perhaps they were intentionally goading him in front of me to embarrass him to a higher degree. Whatever the case, without regard to anything else in the world at the moment, the little guy defiantly took on his provokers by raring back and calling them by the most contemptuous name he could muster. "Ass!" he shouted in full rebellion.

The air was sucked out of the room as the older kids gasped in delight at what he had just said, right in front of the preacher, no less. Yes, the little guy had committed a church house faux pas, but my heart absolutely went out to him at that moment. I might have been tempted to call the pests by the same name had I been in his shoes. I wanted desperately to console him and minister a helping of grace and mercy to the exasperated boy, but he quickly ran off to cry in the arms of his mother.

Having been picked on as a kid myself (then again – who hasn't been?), I was particularly empathetic to my buddy's plight. I didn't want him to ever think that church was a place of condemnation, but rather of mercy and healing grace. There were probably plenty of adults present that day that were hiding far worse secrets in their heart that would have made them run to the arms of mama in tears if revealed to the pastor.

On the afternoon of my young friend's unraveling, as I was pulling into the driveway at the parsonage, another car quickly pulled in behind me. It turns out my buddy saw me heading home, and insisted to his mom that she stop so he could talk to me. Completely of his own initiative, he slowly walked towards me there in the driveway with his head as low as it could hang and arms stretched long at his side. It was his death march of Bataan.

He spoke with an endearing speech impediment not uncommon for a boy his age. "Patter Dweg," he said, "I'm torry I taid a bad wood in chuch."

I couldn't help but smile. I took him in my arms and gave him the absolution that he needed and reminded him that he was loved. Loved by Patter Dweg, and loved by God. He shuffled back to the car and was gone.

After he left, it occurred to me that his sweet little act of contrition was not so much about saying the "bad wood", it was that he had said it in church. I'm not going to parse over his words, because I know that they were genuine and sincere. But I have to laugh that his way of saying them reflects so many adult acts of contrition as well. We're not always as sorry about the offense as we are about the fact that it is made public.

As I scrolled through Facebook, I couldn't help but laugh through the tears as I saw my little buddy, a tall lanky 18 year old flanked by family at his high school graduation, and I remembered again the day he "taid a bad wood in chuch." I lifted him in prayer afresh, uncertain of where his heart is today or what his experiences with the community of believers has been over the years.

Embraced By Mercy

The embrace of those who are hurting, whether by their own misdeed or not, is the end product of a soul made new by mercy. This journey that we're on together needs more people who practice the fine art of imitation - imitating the great mercy of our Father God, and bestowing it as generously as we received it.

In Luke 6, we find Jesus setting the bar for mercy so high that we are to give it even when we've been done wrong by the potential recipient. How could we be held to such an unreasonable standard? How could God actually expect us to show mercy to someone who has perpetrated a vile, cruel offense against us? It's because God is sadistic and unreasonable, right? No, it's because that is the very thing He did for us.

Now, when you and I are in a church building or we're reading a good ol' churchy book, we might be so puffed up and feeling all Jesus-loving and aware of our surroundings to the point that we readily agree that this is just how mercy works, and should work. But how do we respond in the quiet of our hearts when we find ourselves walking beside someone is is hurting and things get ugly and smelly and all earthy?

I grew up in southern Indiana. As a child, I loved it when we walked the creek beds winding through time forgotten hillsides and found these special, ugly looking rocks called geodes. Geodes looked something like a petrified brain on the outside. However, if you crack one open, which is no easy task, you find it full of sparkly, shiny, beautiful crystals. How can something so ugly on the outside be so beautiful inside?

Our problem is often the reverse. How can someone so beautiful on the outside (work with me, people), be so ugly on the inside? How is it that we can walk in God's mercy and be so devoid of it on the inside. I'm not passing out condemnation cookies here; this is my predicament as well.

Let mercy be our life-song. Let mercy be our rhythm and rhyme. Let mercy be the poetry of our soul so that all can find it and sing the song along with us.

Without mercy, there is nothing left to read here, folks. Perhaps this is a good moment for some soul-bearing prayer.

Fruit of the Tree of Knowledge

Another southern Indiana memory is that of the wonderful little fruit called the persimmon. Are you familiar with this? When ripe, it's a deep orangish-brown, and about the same circumference as a quarter. Oh, and the ripe ones lay on the ground. I learned this lesson the hard way as a young boy.

In the fall, mom would make this wonderful concoction called persimmon pudding. It was more like a very moist cake. Her version included a heavenly caramel glaze on top. On occasion, my sister will still make one for my birthday. You could occasionally find persimmon pulp for sale, but most of the time, you have to procure it for yourself.

When picking persimmons, timing was everything, because deer also loved to eat them. As we would labor to pick up the delectable fruit from the ground, I once, and only once, asked my dad why we couldn't pick the more abundant fruit from the tree. Knowing I would need to discover the truth for myself in order to believe it, my dad invited me to pick one and take a bite. I did. And then I puckered. And puckered. And puckered. You see, until they fall to the ground at just the perfect stage of readiness, tree-bound persimmons are the most devious blend of bitter and sour. That day I picked the fruit from the tree of knowledge, and I learned a lesson that I haven't forgotten.

We speculate that the fruit that Eve and Adam sampled from the forbidden tree of Eden was an apple. We don't know this, but it's our time honored traditional explanation. I muse that the fruit was a persimmon. Eve bit it, Adam bit it, and mankind has puckered ever since.

This is not a lesson in original sin, but rather, a reminder that mercy often has to reach farther down and requires much more back bending, but the results are far sweeter. The easiest route is not always the best way. The fruit on the tree seems so much more inviting, but the result is so much less pleasant. Don't be afraid of working a bit harder to be an agent of mercy.

Failure to show mercy can often lead to conflict. Everyone gets bloodied in that battle. Moving to the beat of mercy can often be just the thing needed to bring a sweeter resolution to a bitter moment. The road to showing mercy takes a bit more work, a bit more commitment.

More Potty Words

There really is no such thing as a bad word. Words are neutral. It's their use, the heart, the intent behind them that gives a word its force. Certainly, there are words we avoid using even in reference simply because we know invoking them would be off-putting to some. But it's the look on our face and the vitriol in our speech that inflames and defames.

The path of suffering and struggle is ugly. It can be shaming. Perhaps embarrassing. I've seen the absolute worst come out of some of the best people I've ever known when they breached their toleration point for hurt. Mercy has a way of helping us to see the dark side of pain for what it is, and it allows us to move forward even if we've been the recipient of a violently hurled scorning word.

We are in an age where some believe we should regulate language. On social media, there are countless articles dealing with "What not to say…" in various situations. Then there is the concept of politically correct speech. There are protests over words spoken, and people in high places lose their jobs over things they've said.

Solomon said it. Jesus said it. James emphasized it. The tongue is rooted deeply into the heart. Not literally rooted, of course, but what the tongue says is the overflow of what is in the heart. This may be one of the most important lessons we need to learn today. But what do we do with hard things said and done by the one who is suffering?

Here is where we get to the problem with all those movements to curb speech and to legislate what can and cannot be said. Hurtful words can be a product of a hurting heart. It would be a never-ending search to go back far enough to see who started the chain of painful verbiage.

As a pastor, I've been the recipient of seemingly endless hurtful words over the years. It comes with the territory. When you minister to others, you're bound to step into hurting places. And where there are hurting places, there are hurtful words. Mercy, mercy.

This, of course, is the same whirling dervish we all will encounter the farther we travel into the valley of the shadow of death. It's not always evil that we encounter there. Hurting hearts can produce hurting words. We must be ready for this.

When those undeserved hurtful words come our way, mercy will be our best response. It won't be easy. We'll fail, and even flail our own fiery darts in return at times. As the realization returns to us that we were recipients of much greater waves of grace when Christ took on our hurtfulness, we must also reckon with the fact that the calling to walk with hurting people requires mercy that is beyond our means. Likely, we will also plead for mercy when we realize that there still are hard callouses on our hearts.

Failure to show mercy to the hurting may be difficult to overcome. That is why they are so dangerous. Let us, then, not grow stagnant in our communication patterns with the Father. There is great strength to be found worshipping side by side with fellow believers who are also failing at overwhelming rates to show enough mercy. Deep breath. Holy pause. Be still and know that He is God. Move forward and be a bit more merciful today.

So you know how I just mentioned hurtful words that have been said to me as pastor? Here's where it get's really painful. I wince with waves of disdain for words that I said to my wife, Barbara, over the years that I walked with her. I wish I could take back every single hurtful thing I ever said to her. Thankfully, as I contemplate the hurtful monster I must've been at times in callously responding to her hurt-induced words, I find myself stepping in the freshly fallen dew of new mercies. Every morning they fall anew. They have a way of quenching the fire of my regret. I'm able to move forward, quite a bit wiser, and beautifully schooled in how marvelously God's mercy does its work. If it's true for me, and I believe it is, it's true for you as well. Have mercy on yourself, just as your Father had new mercy on you today.

"The faithful love of the lord never ends! His mercies never cease. Great is his faithfulness; his mercies begin afresh each morning." Lamentations 3:22-23 (NLT)

Write out the words of Lamentations 3:22-23 and place them where you'll see them regularly every day. Spend weeks contemplating these words, and be refreshed by them.

1. How can we put the words of Lamentations to use in dealing with the hurts and hurtfulness of others? Is there a pattern at work in these words that we can also apply to how we deal with those who suffer?

2. Think of times when you've failed to show mercy, and now feel regret. How can the weight of those circumstances make you wiser for this new leg of your journey? Perhaps God is giving you an opportunity today to learn by past failure so that you will be even stronger in the next phase of ministering to the hurting.

3. What is the lesson of the geode mentioned here? How can we apply that to this teaching about mercy?

4. Now think of the persimmon. What can we learn from this strange little fruit that we must let fall to the ground before it's ready to be eaten?

5. Do you struggle with taking offense by words others say? How does it instruct your response if you remember that hurtful words come from hurting hearts?

A blessing prayer for you:

May the Father who is rich is mercy fill you to overflowing with His great healing balm. May mercy flow freely from you as well. May your words grow kinder and richer every day. May we be released from the burden of being offended so that we may love more generously.

Six

YOU ARE THE ANSWER
TO SOMEONE'S PRAYER

Let the title of this chapter soak into your bones for a moment. You are the answer to someone's prayer. You have divine purpose.

I was blessed to be raised by a father who taught me to live with this kind of understanding; one of my highest callings would be to serve others. The sacrificial mindset isn't eagerly embraced by our culture, but it is essential to understanding what it means to walk with Jesus. My upbringing emphasized working hard and giving generously to others.

Dad declared Jesus to be Lord of his life in the early years following his service in the military. One night, driving home from church, dad got a life-changing lesson in what it means to follow Jesus to the side of someone in need.

Dad had joined the military out of spite. He was tired of being told what to do at home, so he enlisted in the Army. That's not the way to go if you want to squeeze out from under the thumb of authority.

Dad breathed a heavy sigh as he recounted watching his mother weep there at the station as his bus pulled away.

After years of service to our country firing Honest John rockets and even doing a tour in bleak Iceland, Dad returned home feeling empty and adrift. Dad's brother, Jack, had turned his life over to Christ and was now attending the Free Methodist Church on the corner of 22nd and Maple

Street in Columbus, Indiana. Uncle Jack became more than a brother, but also a spiritual father to my dad. It was in this environment that my father definitively let Jesus be Lord of his life.

One night after an engaging Bible study, dad put his Bible on top of the dashboard of his car and headed home.

As he approached the vehicle of a motorist stranded at the side of the road, he felt increasingly compelled to stop and help. Though he wrestled with the need at hand, he found it too easy to accelerate on past the car with the flashing trouble lights. The struggle wasn't over though; dad felt no less a sense of obligation even with the car firmly in his rear view mirror. Finally, in yielded obedience to a voice he could no longer ignore, he turned the car around and headed back to help.

He wasn't prepared for the impact this encounter with two strangers, a mother and her son, would make on his life.

As he drove away from the disabled vehicle, passengers in tow, the woman said something that gripped Dad's heart. As she tapped on the Bible sitting there on the dash, she said to her son, "You see, I told you that if we prayed, God would send help."

I still get chills when I think of that, picturing my young dad with his slicked back hair driving what surely would now be considered a classic car.

My dad would live a life full of obedience, often meeting the need of hurting people.

There were those Sunday mornings on the way in to church where we would stop and pick up a van load of people Dad had been ministering to. There were always plenty of hurting souls praying for help, and Richard Fish was willing to do whatever he could.

I'm thankful for that mighty man of God who instilled an important ethic into my life. I'm also reminded that when you follow Jesus to the side of someone who struggles, you may well be the answer to a prayer they had been praying.

Incidentally, Dad would brag that Uncle Jack could always outdo him in acts of mercy. There's the legendary story of the time my uncle assisted stranded motorists from a neighboring state. He dropped everything he was doing to drive them home, hundreds of miles away. Then, of course, he had to turn around and drive the same distance back home, sleeping only a few hours before heading to work early in the morning.

I'm tempted to say that I could never live up to these examples of mercy that raised me, but then helping others is not a competition. I suspect we all have our difficult duties that God sets us to doing as a result of someone's prayer for help.

Made For The Moment

"For we are God's masterpiece. He has created us anew in Christ Jesus, so we can do the good things he planned for us long ago." This is Ephesians 2:10.

There's that much reviled word, "Do."

The word "do" has fallen out of favor with some modern Christian authors, teachers and thinkers. There is a bedeviling fear that doing something might thwart the grace of God.

However, God didn't make you to be a Forest Gump feather floating through the air, or some sort of spiritual amoeba meandering through the sea of life to sweet heavenly shores. Grace propels us into the lives of each other. This is why one of our chief directives from Jesus is to love others. God saw so much value in us, He was so pleased by the art that is alive in us, that He used Jesus to make us just what we need to be to do powerful things. Our free gift of salvation is just what we needed to help us do the good things God foresaw long ago.

I like to think of how God looks at all creation, without the restraints of time that we feel, and sees Moses, me, and future generations all at the same time. Through Christ, He brings all things together. He effects a plan that is bigger than us all but able to touch even the smallest life. As He looks on at all creation from the vantage point above time, God generously allows His Spirit to empower us for work beyond our ability. This is the plan: suffering people would be helped by each other. God is the reason, Jesus is the example, the Holy Spirit is the power. We share the very same force that propelled Jesus out of death and back to life. That's enough to cause those who belong to Him to act with ravenous waves of good deeds for each other, deeds that meet the needs of hungry, praying hearts.

So, in giving us purpose, in providing the power to do good things, He uses us to help those who suffer. As they pray to God for help, God's perfect design for us puts us into play in such a way that a need is met. I get so excited when I think about this! You and I are perfectly equipped to be on Team Jesus. When a hurting plea is sounded, those who are obedient to the way of Jesus will find themselves inexorably drawn to the side of those who hurt.

We are transformative elements placed purposefully into this world to offer relief to the distress around us. We have been empowered, commissioned, and given permission to act mercifully into the life of someone in need.

Are you willing? It is by grace and the power of the Holy Spirit that you are being made ready. You have all that you need in Christ. You are no mere drugstore remedy, but a carefully conceived creation of the Most High.

Moving To Your New House

My sister is so beautifully creative in the ways she has raised her children, teaching them powerful life lessons along the way. Her oldest, Kyle, was still quite young when they moved from their first house to a nicer location that they would now call home. Kyle was old enough that he had strong attachments to the first house. After all, it was the only home he'd ever had.

Kyle was an atypically smily and social young boy. He was crowned with wisps of soft blond hair and illumined by a smile that insisted on warming even the coldest of hearts. By the time he'd made it mid-way through his single digit years, it was time to move to a new address.

Stephanie decided it would be useful to help Kyle make a healthy transition with a fun little game. So she took him by the hand and lead him to each room in the old house to say goodbye.

"Goodbye, kitchen, we've eaten many great meals here in your walls. Thank you!"

"Goodbye, living room. We've laughed in you, shared stories in you, had birthdays and holidays. Thank you, living room, for all the great memories."

"Goodbye, bathroom. We've… well… you know."

Then they approached the hallway that led to Kyle's bedroom, his safe place, his haven. It was his absolute comfort zone. Looking down to gauge his reaction, she noticed Kyle's lower lip begin to quiver, and a tear was welling up in his eye. She realized more than ever the importance of helping him say this goodbye.

With a mother's gentle hand leading him to the bedroom, tears flowing, he was able to say, "Goodbye bedroom. Thank you for being my wonderful place of rest and play."

Fast forward now one hour into the future. They had arrived at the new house with its mad array of boxes and carefully packaged possessions covering vast percentages of the real estate. And Kyle is running, he's laughing, he's joyous in his new bedroom. It's bright, it's big, it's everything he wanted! As he played and explored, the old bedroom slipped into a place of memory. There were no more tears.

I've thought of that story so often as I've contemplated how difficult it is for us to move forward. We like the old. It's comfortable, full of wonderful memories, and it has served us well. Sometimes the old house represents our habits and lifestyles before allowing Jesus to move us to His better way. Perhaps, too, that old house represents the places we were before the struggle began, before the illness set it, before our own personal market crash occurred.

Our job in walking beside those who hurt can often be the tedious task of holding their hand, helping them to say healthy goodbyes to that which will not return, and move into the new phase God has prepared. There may be tears. There may be hesitation. But there is also the glorious, hope-filled vision of what is ahead for those who are in Christ.

This may be the exact role God has in mind for you. You will do so well in it as you continue to say your yesses to His way.

You Are Just What Is Needed

One of the more common things I've had said to me in my role as pastor is, "I could never do what you do." I usually laugh and respond, "I can't do it, either!"

Rare is the person that seems to handle the challenges of ministering to the needy with efficient aplomb. Realistically, it's a job that's too hard for most of us. We simply can't do it. Encouraging, huh?

I do this pastor thing with the full understanding that God's Spirit inhabits, empowers and enhances the work. It's the same privilege available to anyone who follows Jesus to the side of the hurting. Oh, I know, you may well have found yourself there because something awful happened to someone you love. Whatever brought you to this place, you'll find that Jesus arrived before you. That's such a wonderful thing to remember.

Psalm 34:18 reminds us that the Lord is near to the brokenhearted. I can attest that this is quite true. I've seen it over and over again.

So, no matter what means has brought you to the place of helping, perhaps even the person's prayers for rescue brought you there, you come to a place where God's presence is already genuinely, absolutely near. Take another deep breath, another holy pause, and allow Him to activate you as only He can.

I'm not sure how many other pastors have had this experience, but each time I've baptized someone, I've felt more like an observer than a participant. I'm certain that in those moments, I'm a willing vessel inhabited by God's holy presence, used for a sacred task. Perhaps this speaks to the hope you have in coming to the side of someone in need. You don't have to be adequate, you simply need to be available.

We may not be up for the task, but we act in concert with the one who is.

You are just what is needed. Not because you're uniquely qualified (though you may well be), but because God is uniquely able to use you powerfully.

—◊—

Challenge yourself to commit Ephesians 2:10 to memory. Imagine the possibilities of a life that is full of plans from the very one who breathed all creation into being.

1. Do you have a spiritual hero? Is there someone whose influence drew you to Christ, or perhaps made you stronger in that relationship? Think of the important lessons you learned through that person, and consider the impact they might have on your life as you come along beside someone who suffers.

2. How many times have you moved from one residence to another? Are there lessons you learned from the move that can be used as metaphors for helping others who've moved into a new reality due to struggle?

3. Think about the impact that grace has on living an empowered life of doing good things. Has God given you a vision for what you can accomplish through the empowerment of His Holy Spirit?

4. Think of examples from the life of Christ that can help us as we strive to serve others. How does obedience to Christ call us to serve others?

5. Can you recall a time when it was clear that God gave you the strength to do something you were sure you could not do? Are there examples of times when you found Spirit led words that were right for a situation, but were a surprise to you as they came out of your mouth? How does the nearness of God change us in times of service to others?

A blessing prayer for you:

May the Father pour immeasurable graces into your life so that immeasurable grace may flow into the lives of others. May you always know the pleasure of God's hand leading you, and may you constantly be away of His power upon you.

Seven

A WHOLLY
INCOMPETENT MAN

*"It is hard to leave my home, my job, my family… everything
I know and trust… to move to the unknown. God does speak
loudly to me and gives me such peace. I do look forward to it
all and I know it is of God and He will bless it. 'Be patient
and faithful.'"*

It wasn't until the days after my wife Barbara's death that we discovered
a journal she had kept back when I made my transition from radio
broadcasting into full-time pastoral ministry. I had no idea the journal
even existed. After reading her words, my deep respect for her grew deeper.

Making such huge changes in life and geography had been difficult for
her. Dramatic change can be difficult for any of us, but add in the ravages
of illness, and it can become even more overwhelming. I confess that I was
not a good husband to Barbara during that time. You'd think it would be
just the opposite; after all, I was finally saying "yes" to the thing God had
called me to do since I was a boy. Ironically, in those very days when I first
learned how to serve others through pastoral ministry, I did the poorest job
of serving Barbara. I failed her in so many ways. My poor decisions led to
the turmoil in our marriage in later years.

Learning to serve well is a lifelong pursuit. My ability to serve my wife first and all others second was hard won. In figuring out how to meet her needs, I learned how to serve others better. A church leader who barely knew us once told me that I was not fit for the ministry due to the struggles we flailed through together. On the contrary, we found that God made our ministry work even more powerful out of the struggle and strain. Barbara frequently lamented that she thought she did a poor job serving as a pastor's wife due to her limitations. I believe she served even more effectively because of them.

It's interesting how God can use our weaknesses in service to make us more effective servants. Even as Barbara struggled with her place in ministering to others, I was haunted by feelings of incompetence. As you serve others, the enemy will use your failures to discourage you. Don't listen to him for a moment.

The Call

From the time I was young, I felt the calling of God on my life to be a pastor. I remember affirming that to my dad in my tender years. I loved the church that Jesus heads and all of its glorious facets. I was particularly prone to orchestrating makeshift church services for anyone who had the time to endure them.

My cousins still laugh about the unorthodox church services I would lead among us at family gatherings. I won't go into details, but it's a wonder I didn't leave them spiritually scarred for life! They tell stories of commercial jingles that I turned into hymns they were encouraged to sing, full of scatological references that my immature mind found quite amusing.

I fought my calling into ministry. I always loved music and radio, and felt sure this was my life's direction. My favorite stop at the county fair was the booths of the regional radio stations back in the day when the on-air talent was live and local. The announcers looked nothing like I'd pictured them. Many were downright ugly, I thought. I would approach them quizzically, musing, "You don't look anything like you sound."

Years later, during my career in radio, those words would come back to haunt me.

"You don't look anything like you sound." I heard it again and again. And I always knew exactly what they meant. I was a lot uglier than they had imagined me! I believed I had a face for radio, and I suppose I was correct.

In 2000, the time was right for me to make the big move from radio into the heart of the music industry itself. I knew that I had been called to be a pastor, but Barbara and I decided instead to move to Nashville, Tennessee. I had made many crucial connections and felt primed for success. That's what I wanted to do, but it wasn't what God had in mind. Instead, he gave me a pastor who made sure I didn't run away once again. I am thankful for Chet Martin who encouraged me to listen to God's voice rather than my own.

Several miraculous things affirmed that I was to serve others through ministry, and not my own desires of fame through music.

One such thing happened while I was driving down the interstate one day, alone and praying. I found myself blurting out, "God, you don't want me. I am a wholly incompetent man!" This became one of only two occasions so far that I experienced something so phenomenal, skeptics will abound. I know what I heard though. I heard God give me an answer to my statement. And He did so audibly, just as if you and I were having a conversation today.

I had said, "God, you don't want me. I am a wholly incompetent man!" He replied, "I know…"

Stop right there a moment. I know? Really? Thanks much, God, that's really affirming! Yet, it was true, and needed to be affirmed.

Continuing on, God said, "I know, but I am a Holy, competent God." I knew immediately what He was telling me. I wasn't about to do something that I could do under my own strength. No one can. I was reminded that it was by faith and trust in God alone that I could respond to His call.

We are not called to walk beside those who hurt because we are competent, though some of us may well be. We are called because God is competent and powerful and beautiful and able to use us even in our weakness. When He does use it, is can be quite beautiful, despite our personal failures.

An Unexplainable Peace

So, back now to Barbara's mysterious journal. Here's an earlier entry:

> *"This has been a weird time for me. I get excited about everything. …God seems to be chasing me and trying to corner me. I think He is giving me time to come to Him but*

I feel the pressure and soon I know He will absolutely pin me in the corner and not let me go until He has me and I give Him all of me. Tonight He has put on my heart that I can not possibly lead a church and set an example and support people in need if I am not totally His."

And later, this:

"I seem to have an unexplainable peace about things. …Some days I feel so tired and sore. I leave work in tears but God comes and gives me assurance that all is well and (I can) lean on Him more. Whatever comes to us, it comes from His hand. Learn to thank God for everything. Don't thank Him FOR your handicap, but IN your handicap you learn that God's grace is so much stronger than our weaknesses."

Isn't it interesting that as I've struggled to find my place in the role God called me to of serving Barbara first, she was also struggling with her own role of serving others? There's the paradox. Those who are served also serve.

No matter how much any of us struggle or hurt or how much we think we can't go on, I believe great peace comes from learning to serve others just as Christ has called us. I have advised people who are struggling or suffering or hurting to find someone else to serve. Find a need and meet it. Encourage someone else who is struggling. One of the greatest routes to that unexplainable peace is the one that takes us into someone else's life. As we began to focus less on me, and more on them, we find ourselves right where Jesus has already gone.

In Your Weakness, Grace

I love that last line I shared from the journal. "Don't thank Him FOR your handicap, but IN your handicap you learn that God's grace is so much stronger than our weaknesses." You will hear me say this often: Barbara did more with her broken body than many of us do with well bodies. I might also continue that thought by saying I've accomplished more in this life by learning to serve than through any other thing I could have done. That's not to my credit or glory, but a testament to what God's grace does in us when we allow it to prosper despite our circumstances.

I apologize if the word "handicap" doesn't seem to fit today's sensibilities. However, Barbara taught me that there was no word or description that we needed to fear once we allow God to lift us to the highest place of servanthood. Whatever word you attach to your frailty, God can use you right where you are.

In Acts 3 & 4, when the believers fell under threat for preaching the Good News of Jesus, their response was not to pray to be delivered from their circumstances. Instead, they prayed that God would make them bolder. And He did.

Our response to threats to our well being is often, "God deliver me from this thing."

I would never protest a prayer like that myself. But it seems even greater, wiser and stronger to ask, "God give me just what I need to serve you more powerfully today." The greatest healing that can take place is more than physical: the healing of the mind and spirit, the transformation of the soul, is the greatest act of healing. This is the place where we truly learn to serve others and fulfill the call to love through Christ in us.

Even though I've set out to help those who walk beside others who suffer, I am also writing to people who suffer as well. Don't think for a moment that God can't miraculously transform your emotions, your spirit, your whole being into an instrument for helping others in powerful ways. It won't ever be OF you, but thanks to Jesus in us, and we in Him, it will happen THROUGH you. You can do it. I know it's possible. I've witnessed it first hand.

The Great Parties

Ponder this:

> **The greatest party you can ever attend cannot come close to matching the humblest service you can ever do.**

For some reason, we've come to mistakenly believe that the party is the pinnacle of existence. Certainly, the folks in the Bible celebrated some pretty awesome parties. There's nothing wrong with celebration.

However, I've known many folks who back away from an encounter with Jesus because they're afraid they'll have to miss out on a really great party. After all, we all know that those mean ol' Christians are only out to steal our fun. (I have known more than my share of people who exemplify this model - and for them, I am sorry.)

The life in Christ is not adverse to great celebration. For those whose lives celebrate the Good News, we have the greatest reason of all to party. But, culturally speaking, we have celebrated the existential escapism of the party lifestyle. It has become a point of revolt against the Spirit-led life. It doesn't take much time on Facebook to realize that your friends who live the party lifestyle elevate it above all else.

I often wonder if the reason we work so hard to elevate things that are empty and shallow is because there is no other way to give them purpose. You don't see many pictures celebrating the seemingly low estate of servanthood. Perhaps it's because we already know what great value that lifestyle holds. And so, in the end, you or I will never find ourselves at any party that can even hold a candle to the the sense of rightness and peace and fulfillment that the humblest service to others can ever bring.

In our incompetence, even in our "handicap", God does powerful work. You weren't called to serve others because you were able to do it; you were simply asked to allow God to show you what HE can do. And it's far better, far greater than any party you can ever attend, guaranteed.

—m—

Think of the times in your life where you've experienced an unexplainable peace and sense of rightness. What brought on this sense?

1. Think about major transition you've had to make in your life. What things happened to help you know that the transition was the right and proper thing to do? Are there ways that God helped you in those times that can also be applied to the help he brings in the moments where we serve someone?
2. Why do you think people avoid serving others? Do you think that we feel inadequate? Does God ever make us adequate enough to serve? If not, where is our hope?

3. Here's an assignment for you. Secretly plot an act of kindness for someone. Perhaps you can anonymously pay someone's tab at the restaurant (don't forget to tip for them as well). Are there other acts of kindness you can plot and carry out in secret? Pray that God will give you the ability and ingenuity to pull it off. Keep a journal of the occasion if you can.

4. Have you experienced a time when serving someone else helped you to get through your own difficult situation? Why do you think that serving others is, or is not, a good response to our own suffering?

5. It's so much easier to get people to come to a party than to a time of serving others, isn't it? Think about this with your friends and discuss ways that you can plot to do good things for others as a group. Create conspiracies of caring!

A blessing prayer for you:

May the love of God have such an impact on your thinking that you begin to see all things through that lens. May a sense of hope and well-being fill you as you see to the needs of others. May the Father strengthen you and enable you as you serve. May He give you a renewed peace that passes your ability to reason it away.

A LOOK OUTSIDE

Now we look at what it means to lock step with the hurting while maintaining a solid footing. How do we maintain hope and deliver help when outside forces seem to conspire against us?

Eight

THE POWER OF HOPE

Martin's father was one of the premier bootleggers in Illinois. Under the protection of some powerful people, he stilled hootch that gangsters from Chicago came to imbibe and then secret off to some Windy City speakeasy. Though quite young, his little red wagon was loaded with the contraband and he was required to spirit it off to the waiting boats on the Illinois River.

As a soldier in World War II, he contracted malaria an astounding five times, had a severe gall bladder attack once, and was expected to survive none of those. His mother was even notified of his impending death.

As a railroad man after the war, he spent the decades as an engineer on a large, powerful locomotive. On a number of occasions his train collided with vehicles of various sort trying to make it over the tracks in front of the oncoming engine.

He survived all of these, including an incident where he was attacked by a raving mad billy goat who chased him, butted him, and urinated on him.

I was privileged to be his pastor, and to know this wonderful, happy, smiling man who greeted me with hugs and hardy handshakes. He was 96 years old when he passed away.

Martin's life story includes finally finding the right wife who rescued him from wild living and not only met him at the altar of matrimony but also paved the way to the altar of salvation and freedom. While previous marriages only ended in disaster, this one spanned 37 years.

I'm thankful that God dots our lives with redemption stories that remind us that we all have great value and we cannot possibly dampen God's love for us. You see, beyond a life of surviving the difficult, here was a life that ventured in the unseemly for many years. It's a wonder how God pursues us and woos us and then forgives us and gives us the means to forge ahead.

Martin would proudly boast that he was just a "regular drunk" until he married the woman who would stand by him and help him find his true life purpose. He was very proud of the stories of his misdeeds because they showed how amazing grace is. And so it is that no matter how far we've fallen or what stumbling block we think we've placed before a loving God, there seems to be no end to His love and mercy.

Hope is a precious thing. It is the shadow that follows us even on the darkest of days on the dreariest of road. No matter where we go, we cannot shake it. It's just there. It's the promise of a Father who loves His children so much that He found every last one of us worth dying for.

So how is it that we can become good enough to walk well beside those who struggle? And what if the one who struggles seems to be guilty of their own undoing? What if the person is an innocent that was bowled over by illness or disease or circumstance? How do any of us measure up? Can we be good enough for the task?

I'm not good enough. Neither was Martin. Neither are you, no matter how fine a character you might be. But hope says we can have life, and a Savior has paved the way.

Hope tells us that it is never folly to invest love into the life of someone who is hurting.

Hope assures us that we are not wasting our time investing in others.

Even though we share the affliction of flesh, we are found to be remarkably lovable by the very God who created the universe by speaking it into being.

A Reason To Get Up In The Morning

Here's a myth you might be inclined to believe. It's a myth that says you are without value or worth, and that all is hopeless. It says God doesn't care about you, and in fact, has likely abandoned you. You might look all clean and well groomed and shiny on the outside, but inside you've bought into the lie that you are worthless or a failure. This is not an unusual feeling for a caregiver. As we walk beside the hurting, our thoughts can easily become populated with ideas about how devalued life has become. When we see suffering day after day, hope not only can take a backseat, it can often fly right on out the window.

The truth is, God pours his mercy out to us all anew every day. Check this out:

> "The faithful love of the Lord never ends! His mercies never cease. Great is his faithfulness; his mercies begin afresh each morning." Lamentations 3:22-23 (NLT)

That means that each new day brings a new display of our Father's love for us. I'd recommend putting that verse in a place where you can read it first thing every morning. Then, when you go out and see the morning dew on the grass, let that remind you that God's mercy for you has arrived once again.

Lamentations 5:1-22 contains what can be called a prayer for restoration. There's a lot of complaining going on in that passage. We might tend to think that it's not very spiritual to complain or moan or groan, and yet our Scriptures contain a lot of it. In fact, if you ask most people, they might tell you that the book of Psalms is full of praises. Would you be surprised to learn that there are actually a lot more laments than praises there?

So why is this? Why did God allow so many complaints to slip into His holy Word?

The ancients understood something that we've forgotten today. The complaints are consistently answered with reminders of how great God is. Therefore, we have a record that misery and feelings of injustice are not new to us. And just like those from ages past, God is still reliable today to bring restoration and healing to His people. When we regularly see suffering, when we spend day after day at the side of the hurting, we can become full of feelings like these.

Have you ever restored a car or furniture or even a house? Restoration is HARD work, isn't it? However, when the restoration is done, the frustration over the difficult labor is soon replaced by the elation of the "wow".

Restoration is a project that is ongoing throughout the life of a believer. If it *feels* hard, it's because it *is* hard. It takes time, and results can be painfully slow in coming. Still, there are always those point where we can look back over the distance we've traveled and become excited to see our progress.

If you are lamenting, and feeling quite broken and battered, you are a prime candidate for God's restoration.

If you are walking beside someone who is full of grumbling and groaning, you, my friend, are a prime candidate as well.

If joy has left your heart, you are a prime candidate.

If you weep because of things you've done, whether the tears are hidden inside or flowing down your face, you are a prime candidate for restoration.

If you feel sick and weary inside, you are a prime candidate.

If you feel empty or desolate, guess what? Prime candidate!

If the path of helping the hurting has left you in dry, parched misery... well... you know. Candidate!

So what do we do, then? What is the recipe for restoration? Here's a great starting point from scripture:

> "Don't become so well-adjusted to your culture that you fit into it without even thinking. Instead, fix your attention on God. You'll be changed from the inside out. Readily recognize what he wants from you, and quickly respond to it. Unlike the culture around you, always dragging you down to its level of immaturity, God brings the best out of you, develops well-formed maturity in you." Romans 12:2 (Message)

A Recipe for Restoration

Don't focus on what is hopeless, fix your eyes on our true hope. Momentary afflictions can blind us to the truly valuable things.

The recipe we find in Romans 12:2 reminds us that culture isn't the cure. Notice it doesn't say culture is a bad thing, but it can be a homogenizing force, fusing us, merging us, blending us until we're just as flavorless as it is. I just finished watching a biopic about President Teddy Roosevelt. Whether you focus on the man's strong positive characteristics, or his disturbing negatives, you can never accuse him of being bland or culture-driven. Whether you agree with all he accomplished or not, he certainly made a difference.

Making the difference for those we walk beside will take us out of the norm of culture. My own experience in the world of serving one who was dramatically ill often forced me into a different reality than anyone else around me. In the end, though, I'm at peace that I made a positive difference in her life. You can have this same assurance. Don't depend on culture for your reward, don't count on culture as your measure. Instead, focus your attention on God.

In the months after Barbara's death, I fell out of a habit that had become an empowering mainstay in my life. At the encouragement of a friend, I began a routine of lengthy, early morning prayer. There is no way to properly tell of the phenomenal impact that lifestyle of prayer made on my ministry or my ability to serve my wife. However, through the dark hours of grief, I found my commitment to that principle waning, then diminishing altogether. For so long I had fixed my attention on God for the sake of others, but now I found myself needing to refocus on Him for my own sake. Thanks to wise counsel, I realized that my years of serving Barbara had put me in the mode of taking responsibility for the emotions and well-being of others. This was a good thing in regards to looking after the needs of a sick wife, but it did not serve me well when I began to apply it to all other relationships.

I made the mistake of transitioning the hope I had which empowered me to serve into feelings of complete frustration over my inability to make things well for others. It took quite a bit of time in personal retreat, and is still a process ongoing today, to return my gaze to my Savior and off of the culture around me. Yes, even church culture can be stifling and demoralizing!

As I regain my mooring, and reassert my resolve to stand in Christ alone, to be saturated in prayer and punctuated with acts of grace and generosity, I have had to learn anew what it means to fix my eyes firmly on God. Once we find ourselves at this reckoning, the from-the-inside-out work can begin.

And so on weak, bending knees, I am learning to pray again. More everyday. Come with me to the side of the Father, then let's go with renewed hope to the side of those who need us.

—◊—

Write the words of Lamentations 3:22-23 on an index card and place them where you'll see them often. Do the same for Romans 12:2. Read them regularly, repeat them often until you've accidentally memorized them.

1. Do you, or someone you know, have a story of incredible transformation? Has God brought you out of great darkness and into great hope? If you can, write out your story to share with friends and family. Make it a testimony of hope. If you don't know of any such story, begin to ask wise, older, mature believers if they have a story. Help them write it or record it to share with others.

2. How have you royally messed things up lately? What regrets are you caring in your belly? Do you think Lamentations 3:22-23 applies to you? What hope do these words bring you?

3. Have you ever restored anything? Think of the comparisons between what it took you to do the restorative work with what it takes for us to be restored - particularly as we do the hard work of coming along beside those who struggle.

4. Try writing out Romans 12:2 in your own words. Do it as an exercise to understand how the words of this verse can be made personally applicable to your own situation. Perhaps include some specifics of things you are struggling with now.

5. Are you like most folks who claim they hate change? Make a list of all the things in your life that you change regularly, or big things that have changed throughout your life. Do you own the same car you did when you started driving? Do you change your clothes? Why do you get rid of old clothes from time to time? Every changed jobs for something better? As you create your list,

notice how change is not a bd thing, but a necessary part of life. Allow yourself the freedom of praying that God will change you and draw you to maturity in all things.

A blessing prayer for you:

Father, may our hope be renewed! May we be formed into mature beings that are activated to serve well and hope big.

Nine

GRAND SLAMS AND BURSTS OF SUNSHINE

I had completely given up hope.

My favorite baseball team took a game into extra innings, and considering the weakness of their bullpen and their less than exemplary record at that time, I went to bed expecting a loss. Surely their pitching would blow it and their bats would remain cold.

Waking up in the middle of the night, I decided to check the score on my phone because apparently I have nothing better to do at three AM. Much to my surprise I saw that my guys had won by a most peculiar score. They won by 4 runs. In a tie game. And they were the home team. This could only mean one thing: someone hit a walk-off grand slam.

A "walk-off" victory means that in a tie game, the home team scores a run and the game is over. The players walk off the field before three outs are obtained.

So, then I was awake. Wide awake. I began thinking of what I'd missed by not staying up to watch the final innings in the wee hours. I thought thoughts and thunked things about the glory of baseball and its unpredictability. I imagined what it must have been like for the brave souls who remained in the stands after a lengthy rain delay and then into extra innings. I eventually lumbered back into slumberville with the smell of stadium brats wafting around in my memory.

Even in our darkest nights, even when the soul feels the most defeated and without reason for optimism, hope has its way of peaking through like a bright sunburst following the storm. This is the blessing of the one who follows Christ to the side of one who hurts.

I am always pleasantly surprised by the grand slams and sunbursts.

One late evening at a church I pastored, after a long meeting of the leadership team, I was blessed with a blessing: one of the ladies laid her hand on my shoulder and pronounced a blessing over me. I do that often for others, and she wanted to make sure I received a blessing as well. It was a profound and meaningful thing. A grand slam and a burst of sun.

Why are those moments so rare? Reality is that grand slams are hard to come by and require the right confluence of events. Bursts of sun are welcome, but the preceding rain is essential as well. Still I can't help but think we're missing the boat by not providing more of these moments for the people we share space with in life.

The Disney philosophy about providing a perfect experience for every park visitor is so stringent, they even schedule the replacement of light bulbs before the bulb dies. You and I are incapable of providing a perfect life experience for those who hurt. But just a little extra attention to details, a few preemptive lightbulb changes, can make a world of difference. Consider the weight of your blessings, your help, your care and concern in the life of someone whose season isn't going so well. A grand slam and a burst of sun would sure do them good. Go to the plate ready to swing. So how, then, do we do that?

Wrestling With Pigs

Recently, I was invited to join in an interesting online argument. It had all the necessary ingredients: it was inflammatory, provocative, and enticing, with all the charm of a cornered raccoon. But just as I began to form my thoughts on the matter, a more reasoned and wise realization dawned upon me. No matter what I say, nobody's life will be made better. There was no blessing to be had in any argument being made. And just like most, if not all, online arguments (political or otherwise), everyone who enters in loses… just like wrestling a pig leaves everyone dirty.

Before entering the ministry, I spent many fulfilling years in broadcasting. I remember a conversation I once had with an on-air personality who had been invited to participate in a pig wrestling competition at the county fair. He, being the good natured sort, agreed to join in. But just before the competition began, he noticed something quite troubling. Not only was the pit full of mud, but the pigs themselves had added a vile ingredient. He was about to step into a giant porcine potty.

I'm quite certain that our culture is no more feisty or carelessly argumentative than any other throughout history. That doesn't lessen the impact of our delusion that we are making a difference by wresting in the mud of ideology. Most of the time we end up with mud in our hair and between our toes, and the pig slips gleefully from our grasp, happy to be covered in filth.

My epiphany on resolving the matter came recently when I was reminded of truth by two hugging dogs. More specifically, the story of two rescue dogs who were saved from their impending date with a shot of doggy death juice by a last minute adopter. Thanks to a viral picture of the two dogs seemingly hugging, hearts were stirred and the pups found a home.

The story makes the difference. While making an argument might deliver a momentary adrenaline boost to our sense of righteous indignation, it's the story, the picture, that truly makes a lasting impact.

I've experienced this countless times as a pastor. All my well-reasoned pleas and exciting exegesis can never match the impact of a story. After all, stories were the primary oratorical tool of Jesus. I've noticed a clear and definable difference in the impact made by the telling of a story; it's as easily discernible as watching the eyes that are connecting with me as I speak.

I've already used many stories and word pictures to make my points. I suspect they impacted you more than anything else I've said, for better or worse. When using social media, I find myself quickly scanning past diatribe and political spiel. What grabs my attention is an emotionally satisfying picture and a simply stated story. Sometimes they make me laugh, sometimes they bring a tear. Frankly, I can never see enough pictures of soldiers coming home.

It seems right to me that the essence of doing good things to make a difference is the story; it's the picture. You can make all the arguments you care to make to try to encourage the one you're coming along beside to get up and go just one more day, but it's the story that makes the difference.

You can urge them with finally tuned logic and well-honed assertions, and they might occasionally respond. But rescue from the pit of defeat will take a bit more. Stories and pictures help our minds to see truth we otherwise might miss.

As I spent what seemed like endless days at the bedside of my wife while she drew what proved to be her last breaths here on earth, I wanted desperately to make sure she knew how much I loved her. I repeated those words endlessly as I caressed her hands and arms. And then I'd tell her why. I would share a story that was on my heart at that moment. I would recount our days together and the memories that were most precious to me. I told our story. Those were the moments when our eyes connected the most. Those were the moments when the love gained form. Those were the tear-blessed words. The stories made a difference.

You're searching for ways to bring meaning and relevance to your thoughts. Tell stories. Use pictures if you can. You will make a difference.

Who Is On Your Team?

I've come to rely heavily on the process of building teams for success. I put a lot of effort into building leadership teams in the church so that we can improve each other's ability to be finely tuned to the Holy Spirit. In my grief I assembled a small, far-reaching community of individuals that I regularly communicated with to seek counsel in seasons of ups and downs. Privately, as I recognize the importance of accountability, I have an informal team of folks I rely on for counsel, advice and prayer as I struggle with difficult things.

It will be remarkably difficult to be a source of hope, encouragement and fortitude for the one you are walking alongside if you don't have others putting the same resources into you.

In the book of James, we're reminded that the only thing that can spring out of you is that which is already in you. An apple tree won't grow watermelons. Pure water and impure water cannot flow from the same drinking fountain. A monkey cannot write a great novel, and a novelist cannot effortlessly swing from branch to branch by their arms. Of course, it's not always a case of what you see is what you get. Many times we don't know the mettle of a person until it is tested.

We need a healthy community to make us a healthy community

member. We refine each other, we provide prayer and counsel, we sharpen one another. As you do your work serving the one who hurts, don't go it alone. A grand slam would be impossible if others on the team did not first get on base.

Your community will also provide the stories you tell. Sometimes this will be for good reason, sometimes… well… not so much. It's all part of the growth process, and stories give us workable tools to better understand our progress of understanding.

Community also creates conflict and tension. If we merely surround ourselves with sycophants who continuously flatter us and fall in lock-step with every word we say, we will be deprived of the ability to be challenged, to learn and to grow. Navigating conflict prepares us to navigate more conflict. Serving others can be laden with strife, and we need to be stronger than like-minded buddies can ever form us to be.

—✿—

Spend a few moments thinking about the stories that define your life. What events changed you? Who made the biggest impact on you and why? Think about how these stories can be used to encourage others.

1. Plot a pleasant surprise for someone you know who is struggling. Perhaps it's as simple as sending them an encouraging card. Maybe you could pray a blessing prayer over them. Keep it simple, and simply do it.

2. Have you ever gotten involved in a discussion that turned into an argument, and in the end, you felt like everyone had lost? Does the idea that a story is better than an argument make more sense in this light? Think of ways you can encourage others without trying to "argue" them into feeling better.

3. Who is on your team? Can you name three people who seem to possess a special maturity or wisdom that you know you can go to for prayer or counsel?

4. Turn your mind now to three people you know who desperately need encouragement and hope. As you pray for them, ask God to direct you in ways to shower them with mercies. Make a plan for

the week ahead to pray for them regularly. As you pray, recognize that you are empowered to act as an agent of hope.

5. Read the classic, "Practicing the Presence of God" by Brother Lawrence. You'll find this small book to be a quick, easy read. Delight in God's presence, and reflect on his presence in your service to others.

A blessing prayer for you:

May many call you blessed because of the service you do for others. May you be inspired to even greater acts of love and mercy as you grow in wisdom and honor.

Ten

I HAVE NO IDEA WHAT YOU'RE GOING THROUGH

I have eaten in far too many hospital cafeterias for one life. Some aren't too bad. Some should be closed as a service to humanity. Let's just leave it there.

Once while standing at a checkout counter in one such medical dining facility, I realized that the money I had picked up earlier in the day was still in my car. The lady kindly but firmly told me that she could not accept my debit card, but she would be glad to watch my tray while I went to a nearby cash machine. As I made the short trek, I noticed that I was being followed by a rather frumpy elderly lady decked out in a full length fur coat and a gigantic fur hat. She was muttering something about the ills of modern technology.

As I inserted my card and pressed in the PIN, the lady pressed into my side and scolded me with all her vitriolic splendor, "Be a man, carry cash!" With that, she turned to shuffle away.

I came up with some spectacular retorts later, but at the time, all I could think to say was, "It's really none of your business."

Be a man, carry cash.

I can't help but shake my head and laugh every time I recall that weird haranguing I encountered. The frumpy fur lady had no idea what was going on with me. For that matter, I often wonder about her backstory.

What made her think she had the authority to chastise me? She didn't have a clue that my wife had been in the hospital for over two months at that point, and that I was the equivalent of a walking zombie. She didn't know that I had the money, but had absentmindedly left it in the car.

She was very confident that I was a slackard in need of her wisdom so that I could somehow set my life back on the path of virtue.

And I wonder... how many times have I done exactly the same thing to others? Oh, I get that when you and I do such things, we do them with only the purest of intentions, right? Or could it be that we are all guilty of speaking into situations with great self-confidence, when in fact, we lacked sufficient background information. Perhaps more pointedly, we had no business opening out mouth in the first place.

Truth is, we can't be sure exactly what the person we come along beside is truly experiencing unless we've walked with them moment by moment and had the most intimate of conversations with them. Even then, no matter how well we think we know someone, there's always the likelihood that something lies hidden beneath the surface. Earlier I shared with you some quotes from a journal found after Barbara's death that revealed things to me I never knew she had felt. I now wonder how many times I thought I knew what she was going through, and I didn't have a clue. This is truly a vital insight when it comes to how we respond to our hurting friend. We can never fully appreciate the inner motivations behind certain things they say or do. In the same manner, remember that people find you to bit a bit of a puzzle, too! These are the reasons why we deal with grace, mercy and love instead of quick condemnation.

Shouldn't You Be Past That By Now?

Tough confession here. In earlier days of my life, I was a bit critical of those who had lost their spouse and used Facebook or some other resource to memorialize them long after the loss. Ouch, that was hard to admit. But I have to do it. I have to let you know that I've been just where many of you have been... quite sure that someone else should be "doing better" in the way they express grief or suffering.

Today, I cringe when someone suggests that there is a set number of days after which a person should no longer grieve. A wise counselor once told me to expect that the "year of firsts," that is, the first year after a loss, will keep the wound fresh and raw.

Having walked beside a very ill wife, I am set on edge whenever someone suggests that someone else should deal with their hardship in a different way. After I lost Barbara, I was overcome by the idea that I should go to every grieving spouse I'd ever walked beside as pastor and apologize to them. I had no idea of what it was really like to experience such a thing. You don't have to lose a spouse to empathize, but be careful of supposing that you know what it's like until you've walked that road.

In the same manner, no matter what the means of hurt, suffering and struggle is in the one you walk beside, rest assured that you only have the bleacher seat. Fortunately we can helpfully empathize and support others in their struggle without ever having experience the depth of any particular situation. To do so requires a great deal of humility and the ability to listen more than we speak.

The Common Denominator Is Pain

We have all experienced great pain. We have all been hurt greatly.

When I encounter someone who is behaving in a hurtful fashion, I remind myself that they are only acting out of their own hurt. This doesn't excuse bad behavior, but it does frame my own response. When I'm open to fair introspection, I freely admit that I, too, have hurt others. I didn't plan to hurt them, and I didn't want to hurt them. But functioning out of my own hurt blinded me to the damage I was doing.

The abuser has typically been abused, the hater has been hated and the bully has been bullied. We all have had our trust smashed to smithereens. Let me be clear that I am not proposing that bad behavior get a pass. However, we need to keep it plainly in mind that there is more to our decision making patterns than meets the eye. There is a certain level of humanity that we all share. Pain in the common denominator.

Now let me bring this back to how we walk beside someone who is suffering or struggling. Keep in mind that their behaviors are born from something you already understand: pain. This is true on so many levels. Many of us can readily quote Romans 3:23 which reminds us that we've all sinned and fallen short of God's glory. This verse comes on the heals of the reminder that God does for us what we cannot do for ourselves. Knowing that we could not possibly atone for our own sinful deeds, He freely did for us what we could not do through the sacrificial death of Christ.

Since we are following Jesus to the side of those who suffer, the onus of having to understand perfectly has been removed and we are free to commiserate out of what we share together. We all likely have something we cannot bear ourselves, and we all have the availability of a Savior who has made the way to wellness possible. Just as salvation is a remarkable gift, so is the way Christ makes it well with our souls in regards to all level of hurt we experience. We share the same guilt, the same ability to mess things up, the same propensity to pain.

When you walk beside someone who suffers, don't presume to know what they are going through. Rather, gently make yourself vulnerable to their needs because you have walked in hurt as well. You don't have to have answers for their details, your care for their pain is sufficient.

Listen Anyway

It's hard for us to listen well. We are so geared towards trying to solve each other's dilemmas. In the days when the heaviness of Barbara's impending death was thick in the air, my good friend and fellow pastor, Steve, came to visit. He sat quietly and listened.

Steve has a special gift for pastoral care that sets him apart from many. He has the gift of ministering to those in the hospital like few I've known.

I made small talk there among the others who'd joined my vigil. I gave little thought to the things I said, among which was my frustration over forgetting my fingernail clippers and dealing with a broken nail.

At some point I realized that Steve was no longer in the room, and I assumed that he had gone back to look in on Barbara. When he returned, he quietly handed me fingernail clippers that he had just purchased at the gift store. It was an inexpensive gift that held the value of gold. My friend had listened, had cared, and had acted.

Be careful not to drown your ability to hear the needs of the one who hurts with your own need to talk. You are not alone in this struggle; it's hard for us all. But God gives the grace to be a help rather than a hindrance, and the gift of listening is one of the truly great gifts the Holy Spirit brings to those who are willing to receive it.

Read Galatians 5:22-23 and observe the list of things that proceed out of the actions of one who abides by the Spirit. Love, joy, peace, patience, kindness, goodness, faithfulness, gentleness, and self-control; each one a grace that could be ascribed to a listener.

I understand that you've heard much about the need to listen well and speak with restraint. I don't remind you of it because it is a new concept; I remind you of it because it brings great freedom to us all. Just as the results of that which is fueled by God's Spirit releases us from the burden of our flesh, so does listening release us from the burden of having to say the right thing. The patience to listen, process and hear what the struggler is saying will guide us to act.

The Middle Child Syndrome

My niece, Alyssa, is a middle child. She is certain that she gets lost between the stories of her older brother and younger sister. Whenever the family remembers a compelling story about one of her siblings, she's likely to ask, "What about MEEEEEE?!?!"

I tell you this knowing that she will glow just to have ANY story shared about her.

OK, so here's one. When Alyssa was small, she loved hats to the extent that anything that would sit on her head would suffice as a hat. Once she actually wore bubble wrap she found laying around.

The thought of being left out can be crushing. If the one you walk beside is struggling, part of that will likely include feelings of being left out. If their mobility is limited, if money is an issue, if they have a problem or a fear that isolates them from others, then they are feeling left out. Struggle is a breeding ground for Middle Child Syndrome, even if someone is not a middle child.

Those who suffer and struggle often have heart needs that get overlooked. My need of something as simple as fingernail clippers was small in comparison to the other weighty things I was dealing with. But receiving the gift of clippers from my friend was huge. His great gift was listening and caring.

I'm sure every middle child nodded in agreement with the idea that they get overlooked in favor of the gold and silver child. The middle child gets the bronze and quickly fades into the woodwork. In suffering, those attention grabbing "siblings" could be things that are physical or emotional, or problems financial or legal. Humanity can easily be lost laying in a hospital bed. Your challenge is to restore the humanity by listening, learning and acting.

—⚏—

Read Galatians 5:22-23 and reflect on how those virtues describe the spiritual gift of listening. This would be a great opportunity to pray that God's Holy Spirit would empower you to fruitfully listen to those in need.

1. Have you ever had an experience where someone belittled or scolded you even though they clearly did not have all the facts? Now, can you think of a time you did that to someone else and later learned that you were sorely mistaken on the details? What lessons can you take from those encounters that will empower you to view the struggles of others with more grace and fewer comments?

2. Do you agree with the idea that understanding that we all share the common denominator of pain unites us all even though our means of suffering might be different? What lessons have you learned from your pain that can help you be a more engaging, thoughtful friend to those going through different kids of pain?

3. How would you rate your listening skills? Do you find that you are frequently thinking about other things while people are talking to you? Do you believe that God is big enough to help you with this problem? Perhaps you can move towards helpful transformation by spending time in quietness before God. Instead of talking to him, listen. What things are going through your mind? Make note of them and turn those things to prayer and action.

4. We are good at creating ministries where we talk to others, teach others, or share with others. What would a church ministry look like that is designed to find ways to listen to others and meet their needs?

5. "Humanity can easily be lost laying in a hospital bed." Think about that statement for a while then create an action plan for how

you can be a part of acknowledging and restoring the humanity of the hurting when they most need it.

A blessing prayer for you:

May the Father inspire you with a great vision for helping those who hurt. May He open your ears so that you have a great depth of understanding. May He open your heart so you have the unlimited resource of compassion.

Eleven

SIMPLE

Yes, you're right, I'm much too young to be a grandfather. Thank you for noticing.

But since I am so marvelously youthful and yet a grandparent, I have gladly embraced the role with gusto. If I'm gonna be a grandfather, I'll be the funnest, bestest pa pa around.

Sadly, my toddler grandchildren live at a bit of a distance from me. That's why I bless the modern technology that allows me to do a video call with my grandchildren every Sunday afternoon. FaceTime, you are divinely inspired!

I have learned some very interesting life facts from my precious little ones. Things like, a fake mustache is comedy gold. The level of amusement and conversation that ensues when Pa Pa appears with a fake mustache is beyond measure. It doesn't even have to be a particularly good fake mustache – just roll with what you got and hilarity will ensue.

Then there's this: just say the word, "bellybutton," and shirts WILL come up. There seems to be a mystical fascination with that special little dimple in their midsection. So much so that the very speaking of the word bellybutton causes shirts to immediately fly up for both of them. Hopefully, and with much prayer and counseling, they will one day overcome this proclivity.

Of course, anyone who has ever dared to entertain a toddler knows that once is never enough. If it's funny once, it must be repeated ad nauseam.

I've learned that crackers are highly addictive baby drugs. There is no finer dining anywhere than you can find in a package of fish-shaped, cheddar crackers. There is nothing more grating on the system of a young one than when the crackers are gone and the D.T.s set in.

The term, "big wet sloppy kiss" was actually invented because of toddlers. Enough said.

I've learned that you don't need music to dance. The beat hits your head, rock the groove. Not recommended for adults in public settings, but it works for kids.

Blissful joy can turn to horrifying shrieks in .002 seconds. Got mood swings?

And when all else fails, make animal noises.

Enjoying young children is one of life's simple pleasures. You just watch them, and they'll provide the entertainment. We needlessly complicate life, but God provided great beauty, great laughs, and great joy in the simplest things.

I am confident that despite our ability to muck up the works, God can restore us in simple moments of prayer and make us right and ready for the walk that leads us to the side of those who hurt.

You can do it. Really, you can.

I began this journey with you by acknowledging that others have expressed admiration for the manner in which I cared for Barbara over the many years of her illness. I am humbled by this, but I also realize that it was as simple as being present and doing my best to do what was right moment by moment.

When I'm video conferencing with the grandbabies, I just hang out. I just have fun. I just do whatever comes naturally. Most of all, I enjoy them, admire them and love them deeply.

I can't imagine a better formula for setting your heart to doing what is right for someone in need. It's really a natural process. You do what you have to do to survive the moment. But, in doing it, you soak the survival method in love.

As you think of the person in need, admire them. Really. Do it. I'm quite serious. Learn to see all the great things about them that God sees.

Think of all the great things they've done, or that they do. If you draw a blank on that one, imagine the potential for greatness (or, even better, true goodness) that rests within us all. That potential is Christ, you see. He is our goodness, He is our measure of great worth. See that, and you'll find something admirable about everyone (even if they themselves have yet to engage with Jesus on any level).

Ultimately, the old adage holds true. The best thing we can do for each other is simply to be there. You can do this. I know you can. It's the power of Christ in You, the same power that raised Jesus from the dead.

Good Enough

I love those mornings when I'm greeted by text message videos from my daughter. One especially glorious day, my little grandson and granddaughter each took their turn telling me they loved me. The words were lavish in their simplicity. The youngest shot off a few rapid-fire, "Hi, pa pa's" followed by sounds that, when properly translated, mean, "I love you."

I could almost see the smile on Barbara's face all the way from Heaven, and hear the words she would say, "Jackie is such a good mommy." She was right, of course. And still is.

May I remind you to stop striving for greatness and reach for something better? Goodness. Be good.

Good uses every opportunity and mode of technology to do good.

Good takes the time to express itself.

Good rescues the lost and saves the desperate.

Good shines its truth in all of God's creation.

Good shuns the political for the poetic and the divisive for the divine.

When God surveyed the works He had created, He pronounced them to be good.

There is simply something good about good.

Your most satisfying moment today may well be taking the opportunity to stop reaching for greatness and do good things.

And may this day be good for you as you do good. Those are the things that will last. It's that simple.

This is your opportunity to simplify. Begin a plan to throw away what needs to be thrown away, and to donate those things you are no longer using. Simplify a room, simplify your heart.

1. What things had you once put off, only to discover that they weren't nearly as hard as you thought they would be. How can this frame your thinking in regards to walking along beside those who struggle?
2. Make a list of things that clutter your life and your schedule. Begin the process of dismissing the unnecessary in favor of creating space for generosity towards and concern for others.
3. If there is a line or two from that last section speaking of what "good" does, write it on a card and place it somewhere you'll see it often for a few weeks. Remind yourself often to simplify, and simply take time for what is good.

A blessing prayer for you:

Dear Father, may your goodness be a part of our fibre. Inspire us to love in a way that makes time. May we be motivated to clear the clutter. Let goodness rain over us and reign in us.

Keys to the mint

Twelve

KEY TO THE MINT: UNDERSTANDING MORE ABOUT GRIEF

In the early days after losing Barbara, I experienced grief in ways I never thought possible. I never knew that a heartache was a real, actual pain you felt in your chest. I didn't realize that things you once took for granted could become triggers for tears. And in those days, I wrote a lot. My heart began to pour out in words, poems, songs.

From the start I vowed that if I had to experience such a great level of pain, I would learn something from it. I became determined to put my grief to work as an agent of healing for others. With that in mind, I will share with you one very raw poetic work I created that I think really emblematically captures the depth and solitude in which grief often manifests itself:

In the stillness of your stillness
By your side there on the way
There was a peaceful draw of strength
At the ebb of each long day.

Those unstrained sighs of joy;
How opulent the frame
The simple understanding
That we both were the same.

How endless are the hours now
Without a pause with you
Where words were never needed
And every word was true.

I settle in for winter
As springtime takes its place
Warmed unhandily by knowing
The smile now on your face.

In the stillness of the stillness
Looking out across the way
I take a halting breath of life
At the surge of this new day.

The Unwanted University

I still get those weird dreams where I've somehow been transported back to my college days. I find out that part of my college career was a sham, and I have to retake my least favorite courses, in whatever I wore to bed that night. Please tell me I'm not the only one who dreams like that. Anyone?

Grief is a strange, unwanted university where the learning curve is steep and you can't help but feel completely exposed to the world as some mortally wounded creature. The superfluity of advice and well-meaning comments can leave us wondering if we've been transplanted directly into insanity. Our community is unsure what to do with a grieving person. Outside our dilapidated, over-used platitudes, we are at a societal loss for words. This is why I've decided to dedicate a chapter to the topic of grief. I am not credentialed in this field, but I have learned a few things that are worth sharing.

As we walk beside the one who grieves, it's likely we'll lose patience with them far too quickly.

I often say that I'm not sure what the manual is for this part of my journey.

There is no playbook, no instruction matrix telling us what exactly to expect, and what is really normal. Thankfully, as I've navigated the grief minefield, I've gotten connected with several very wise friends who've traveled this road before me and have helped me to stay grounded. The universal truth learned by each of us seems to be that you can't begin to imagine what it is like unless you're there yourself. To a degree I've become quite cynical of anyone offering advice who hasn't actually experienced this kind of loss personally. Cynicism aside, though, it is far better to seek help from someone who can't fully understand what you're going through than it is to struggle in solitude and eventually succumb to the pain.

The most certain thing I can say is that it is different for each of us. My faith is certainly shaping this struggle. My years of experience as a pastor has helped. Having the right friends and a supportive community means the world. I'm also learning that I'm much stronger than I realized. Couple that with years and years of preparing for this thing (even though you can never be prepared for the breadth and the width of grief), I sense that I have a lot of plusses working in my favor.

Still, I'm plagued with this idea that I ought to go back and apologize to anyone I've ever counseled who had lost a spouse. I had no idea what they were actually experiencing. I saw it in 2D, but now live it in 3D. Grief has a depth, a physical reality that is unlike anything else I've experienced. I've been to the dark low places, and I'm thankful that I had the friends, the spiritual grounding, and the motivation to not let the low spots bury me. If you're going through those dark moments, inhabited by some very vexing dark thoughts, please know that you're experiencing what the rest of us out here have gone through as well. I would encourage you to create a network of friends who've been through the same kind of grief you're experiencing. Don't be afraid to engage with a qualified counselor. Find a means of expressing your grief (like I have done in my writing); discover an artistic or creative or constructive way to express your struggle.

What You Need To Know About My Grief

I have compiled a list of ideas that should be useful as you come along beside someone in grief. These things will most certainly vary from person to person, but I suspect that they will give you some seeds for thought that will help you to understand their world a bit better. Here are things that I experienced that may well share universal truth with others who grieve.

1. I'll talk when I'm ready.

In the aftermath of Barbara's death, I lost track of just how many invitations I received to talk if I needed. It would usually go like this, "Call me anytime if you need to talk." I greatly appreciated the offers, but I soon realized that it was a statement akin to, "If there's anything I can ever do, just let me know." I can't tell you how much I appreciated the offer when it came from friends - I understood the depth of concern behind the offer. However, when it came from strangers, I found it to be a bit disconcerting.

Here's what you need to know. I couldn't predict when the words would come pouring out, but there were also times I simply didn't want to talk. The secret is having presence. I would not seek someone out, but if they were with me at the right time, I would often bear my soul. I've found this to be a common sentiment among grievers. You don't need to ever offer yourself as a potential listener. Just be there, and be ready.

2. I feel like the third wheel.

I spent over 25 years being married, and learning to socialize without my partner was surprisingly difficult. I felt like the guy with a black eye and a swollen lip. It seemed like everyone knew I'd been beaten up, and they're not sure how to make me feel better.

I've heard from friends who've remained single long into adulthood that feeling like a third wheel can be a problem for them as well.

The solution isn't to avoid the friend in this position but to seek out ways to make them more at ease. Perhaps invite them along with small groups of friends rather than couples. For me, having the occasional guys-night-out with friends of all ages helped me greatly. The most important tip here is to make sure you're not avoiding your friend for fear of not knowing what to do with them.

3. Invite me.

Sure, I felt like the third wheel, but that didn't mean I wanted to do nothing. I wish I had one of those kinds of personalities that I could just show up at someone's doorstep like many invited me to do. I wish I could be Mr. Social and find ways to get "out there" and dance. That's not me. On the other hand, I didn't much care to be stuck at home with my loneliness.

So, rather than an open-ended invite, keep in mind that if you call and invite your grieving friend over, that may be just the push they needed.

Let me add a word to those who are grieving, and receive such an invitation: Go.

After I helped my community understand that I needed invitations, I began to receive them. Often, I would find myself preferring to sulk rather than to take up the offer. Each time, though, I could hear Barbara's voice in the back of my mind telling me I'd better accept the invitation or they would stop coming. So, I went. And every single time I went, I felt better. I had good times, good conversations, and good camaraderie.

Please go. You won't regret it.

4. Don't be afraid of what I say if I do choose to be vulnerable with you.

Those who find themselves grieving are often amazed at just how deep and devastating the finality of death really is. They discover that there are five million opportunities for missing their loved one. They are often surprised to learn that grief really IS a physical experience.

Here's the deal. Your friend needs to be able to tell you how they feel without the fear that you'll overreact. The journey can be hard enough without them having to console you as well. Let them be honest with you without feeling you need to scold them or counsel them. Just listen.

5. Listen and learn.

Since I help people for a living, I've used my awful experience as an opportunity to learn. I found it made me more compassionate and empathetic. One BIG thing I discovered is that you can learn so much about how to help someone who is grieving simply by listening to them. I found myself inadvertently tipping off what my heart was most needing in the moment. I also started to hear others who were hurting do the same thing. Rather than spending their talk-time thinking about what you're going to say next to soothe someone, hear what they say and use it to know what they need most in the moment.

In the process of creating, and releasing these ideas on social media, I discovered that there were a few professional counselors who strongly disagreed with some of what I had to say. Keep in mind that I am not advocating a plan for the grieving here. I'm simply offering some simple tips for how the average person can best meet the needs of the person they're coming along beside through this process. As a follower of Christ, I also advocate prayer and then more prayer as you learn to love the one who struggles.

Trigger days

I don't know if there's a medical term for it, but I've taken to using the term, "trigger days," for certain, specific days that seem to bring me to grief. If you're not aware of this common phenomenon, then you've come to the right place.

There have been certain points in time where the grief over the death of my wife seemed amplified many times over. Mother's Day was a major trigger day. Family birthdays. Holidays, of course.

On a trigger days, I could count on the first few teardrops to open up the floodgate.

I am so embarrassed to admit (but will do so for the sake of growth) that there was a time when I had little patience for someone in grief who didn't seem to me moving on quickly enough for my personal comfort. There they were, doing just fine, then all of a sudden, they were in the pit of despair. Perhaps it was my own feelings of inadequacy to console them at such times that led me to long for the simpler explanation for solving their funk.

Now I've come to understand that grief is a lifelong process of learning to live with and around the emotional debris of loss.

Here are three quick things you should know about your friend's trigger days:

1. One bad day doesn't mean every day is bad.

There is a phenomenon in radio broadcasting known as "FM skip" that will occasionally allow an FM broadcast wave, which bounces from the ground to the atmosphere, to find a place where it can bounce extra high and land outside of its usual reach. If you've ever received a strange FM signal from much farther away than usual, one that only lasts for a short period of time, that is FM skip.

Grief can surprise you in a similar manner. You think it's far away, but for spurts of time, it bounces in from the atmosphere. Thankfully, those days pass and you get back on your feet again.

2. There will ALWAYS be "those moments" for the one who grieves.

The unanimous consensus of all those who grieve, especially in regards to losing a spouse, is that deep grief will pop up even years into a new, happy marriage. This fits in well with the concept that you never stop grieving the loss, but you do learn to live around it. Death does not have to consume us; in Christ, we have victory over it. It's perfectly natural to hurt, but it is not healthy for that pain to consume you every day.

If your grief overwhelms you day after day, even as time progresses, that is a red flag that you deserve to have some good help from an outside source.

3. Maximize the joy triggers.

There are things that will invariably bring a smile to your face and a warm, nestled feeling to your heart. For me, it's thoughts of my grandchildren. I have plastered my walls with plenty of pictures of them to remind me of what a great treasure life still is.

I also find my job to be a joy trigger. Granted, there are moments when even the best job stabs away at your emotions. For the most part, I find great comfort in accomplishment and doing things that make the life of others better.

Even if you despise your job, it's almost certain that the work you do benefits someone in some way. If you think about it, your work, no matter how menial or demeaning it might seem at times, is most certainly a blessing to someone. Without you, and the things you do, someone would be lacking the good thing you help provide. That's right, you ARE a blessing! Remember that. Make it a joy trigger.

Take a moment to ponder the ideas expressed here and compare them with your own grief experiences. Were there specific things mentioned here that particularly resonated with the experience you've had in grieving a loved one's death?

1. What revelations have come to you from your grief experiences that you can use to make you better at helping and encouraging others? Had you previously considered that the great depths of pain you've felt - depths that at times made you feel so alone - were learning opportunities to help you understand the experiences of others in a more helpful, useful way?

2. We all are slaves to our busy lifestyles. Is there any level of busyness that is so important as to keep us from inviting a hurting person to participate in a life event? Why do you think our priorities often tend to be more self-focused? What, then, would be the Christlike response to these things?

3. Is there a meaningful way that your social groups can create opportunity for listening? How can we do this without being contrived?

4. Have you had experience with "trigger days"? How can understanding our own triggers help us to better minister to the needs of others who experience their own, unique triggers?

5. Plot ways to maximize "joy triggers" in your community group. How can you maximize the joy that others experience through strategic joy triggers?

A blessing prayer for you:

May the Father in Heaven bless you with an extraordinary sense of the joy we have in Him, may it overflow generously into the lives of others.

Thirteen

KEY TO THE MINT: HOSPITAL VISITS

Problem:

I'm going to visit a friend in the hospital. Is there anything I should do for the loved one or friend who is coming along beside them?

Solution:

Just because we're focused on the person who is in that hospital bed doesn't mean there aren't real needs present in the loved one, family, or friend who is by their beside. It can be a struggle to know just what to do for the ones looking after the needs of someone stuck in a hospital. I've spent so much time caring for loved ones in hospitals that I've often joked that I've earned my junior medical degree. So, take it from me, you can't go wrong showing love and servanthood with any of these ideas.

1. Bottled water.

Hydration in the hospital is essential, yet difficult. Many times, nurses and other caregivers will bring water to family members. However, the reality is that the patients are first priority, and there are days when even the medical staffer most in tune to the needs of the family members or friends present may not have the time or ability to serve in this way. Taking along a nice sized, but portable bottle of good quality water can be a real blessing.

Tell your friend, "I know that good hydration is difficult here, so I hope this will help." This might help to trigger in them a reality that they hadn't considered. Hospitals are a good place to get sick! Drinking plenty of fluids is a good starting place in the endeavor to not become the one in the bed.

I fully understand that there are many different perspectives on the use of bottled water, but I believe this is a tenable solution to a real problem. For less than five bucks, you can make a quick stop at a convenience store near the hospital and procure a cold bottle of good quality water that will speak love and concern into the heart of the receiver.

2. Soft tissues.

Frankly, the stuff at the hospital feels like it's made of sandpaper. Very thin sandpaper.

If you're visiting a family where the illness is quite serious, it's probable that emotions are running high and many tissues are being used. This is the place where it's especially good to bring a box or soft package of tissues. Stick with the plain, soft and substantial variety; it's advisable to avoid the medicated or coated tissues in this instance.

3. Dining out.

Hospital food can get very expensive day after day. Not to mention that, depending on the location, the food may not be all that pleasing to the taste or the digestive system. I've been in hospital cafeterias where it seemed like the vegetables were not only complete unseasoned, but they seemed to actually repel salt! I've made the mistake of believing that something called "turkey loaf" would be both a healthy and tasty selection. Even the best cafeteria can become unsavory after a time.

What a blessing it has been for me when a friend has arrived and offered to take me out for a meal. I understand that some folks may feel compelled not to leave the hospital, but I believe that this is an offer worth making.

Personally, when somebody offers to take me out, I feel a bit uneasy suggesting the place to go not knowing what their budget is. So, I recommend that you have several good alternatives in mind to suggest. Also, make it clear from the start that you're buying, and make sure that you've selected a place where you can afford the most expensive options should the recipient be one that sees this as an opportunity to order lobster (I'd like to say that this would never happen, but…).

4. Listen to what they say they need, but don't ask them what they need.

I know it's easy to ask – and it shows cares and concerns. But I've found if you listen long enough, people will tell you what they need.

We've already dealt with the need to listen, but it's a reminder we cannot hear enough.

5. If you can, offer to stay with the one in the hospital.

Assuming the one admitted to the hospital could use some reassuring company, and that you are sensitive to their needs, this can be a wonderful relief to a family. You'll find that in most cases, especially where the loved one is admitted long-term, the family just might appreciate being able to take care of things at home for a while.

There are so many important variables to this option, but let's just assume that you're wise enough to navigate those well.

One final heads-up. A longer visit doesn't mean you care more.

Many times a short visit is just what the doctor ordered for a tired family. If you don't share a close bond with the family you are visiting, then a respectfully quick visit is appropriate. Don't feel the need to entertain them or offer scintillating conversation. I've been in awkward situations where someone has visited and I've felt like I needed to carry the conversation or entertain them in some fashion. Staying longer doesn't mean you care more.

A Word About Hospital Staff

Perhaps I am biased on this because I have known so many hospital workers over the years, but you need to remember that they are not your enemy. Just like any other professional, there will be good ones and bad ones and those in between. Fostering a good relationship with your nurses and other caregivers is crucial to getting the best care possible. Granted, when the health of your loved one is at stake, there is little room to tolerate carelessness. Suffice it to say that if you're around hospitals and medical professionals, you will hear horror stories on both sides. Rather than dealing with patient rights, and in hopes of avoiding any of us becoming crusaders against anyone in scrubs, let me offer a few practical things you can work into your conversation with the medical professionals that will help foster better relationships and, I believe, better care. This falls under the category of controlling the one thing we truly can control - ourselves. I approach these realizing that some of you will be resistant to these ideas, but experience tells me these are great tools I can use to help make the relationship more productive.

Acknowledge that you know the staffers are extremely busy.

Thank them repeatedly. Let them know you appreciate what they are doing.

Use courtesy. "Sir" and "Mam" are not out of fashion. Address them by their title as a sign of respect.

Smile. Really... it works.

Always remember that you are in a professional healthcare environment. It is not their job to give you hotel or restaurant quality service.

Speak lovingly of the patient. Let the staffers hear you speaking well of the one they are serving.

Don't be argumentative or foul-mouthed. This will only make things worse, guaranteed. Instead, if you believe their is a problem, seek out a superior and speak to them. Be courteous and civil to them as well and you will get a much better response.

Let them know you are praying that God will give them the strength they need to serve today.

Greet them kindly and quickly at the beginning of their shift. Introduce yourself so they know who they are dealing with.

At the end of their shift, thank them and bless them.

Don't occupy their time with stories or long diatribes. Keep it simple.

—ɯ—

Create your own personal list of hospitality solutions for hospital visits. Share them freely on social media if you participate in that medium.

1. Discuss thee ideas with off-duty medical professionals you may know. Get their feedback and grow in wisdom.
2. Create a savings envelope where you occasionally stash a few dollars to use in services such as I've suggested when doing hospital visits.
3. What kindnesses have you found to be of greatest value when others have served you in the manner suggested in this chapter?
4. What does the Bible say about hospitality? Spend some time looking for passages that address hospitality and use those to challenge your thinking as you serve others.
5. You have likely had both good and bad experiences in hospital settings. What advice have you found to be most valuable in creating a better, more positive healthcare environment?

A blessing prayer for you:

Father, bless those who serve in healthcare with your heart, your compassion, and your healing strength. Fill our minds and souls full of great ideas for serving others, and may Your love be evident as we do so.

Fourteen

KEY TO THE MINT: FUNERALS

Problem:

I'm never sure what to say to someone at a funeral. I reach for some clumsy line that I'm sure came off sounding like a cliche'.

Solution:

I like to joke that finding the proper way to express your true love and concern in a funeral situation is the true holy grail of social dialogue! That may be a bit of an over-statement, but it contains elements of truth.

All too frequently we're at a loss for words when someone is grieving and we want to console them. Our mind desperately reaches for something comforting and inspiring, but all that seems to come out is, "Let me know if there's anything I can do."

Let me give you some good news. Most people you've attempted to console have no real memory of what you said. They only remember that you were there.

That's my experience. Having gone though the whirlwind of grief for both parents and a wife, I remember little of what was said to me. I DO remember the people that were there, those who called, those who sent cards. Those memories are precious and sustaining. I remember hearing the "anything I can do" line repeated continually, but I accepted it as a sign of love; my friend was grieving with me and at a loss for words.

There is a well worn list of lines we seem to exercise repeatedly. There are too many people out there creating "what not to say" lists, and I don't want this to degenerate into verbal policing. Your presence and compassion will heal over a world of bad word choices.

However, if I could be so bold, I will humbly recommend that you never say:

"God must've wanted them worse than we did." (cringe, cringe, cringe)

Now that we've resolved that, let's move into the positive realm. Here is the secret to always having the right thing to say when consoling the grieving. It's almost too simple. Tell them WHY you love them, or WHY you love the one who has passed.

If you knew the departed, start thinking in advance about what made that person so special to you. Do you remember a short, uplifting story – especially one the family might not know? Can you affirm the positive influence this person had in your life? What did you like about them?

Let's say you're friends with someone in the family and didn't really know their deceased loved one that well. Turn your words of affection to the one you've come to console. Tell them how much you love them and why. Remind them of why they are so special to you.

Brevity is the key. If the one you're consoling takes initiative to continue the conversation, then allow them to do that. The consoler, however, should be quick, sincere, and considerate.

The greatest thing about this solution is that you really don't need to say much of anything at all. Remember, it's your sincerity and your very presence that will speak the loudest. Most of the time, silent eye contact from a compassionate face, a hand on the shoulder, and a shared quiet moment says it all.

Make a list of things that love does and doesn't do. Use this as your helper in accomplishing what is suggested in this chapter.

1. Why do you think people use clumsy, cliched lines when addressing people who are hurting? How can a better knowledge of scripture help us in the things we say to others in times of grief?

2. Create a plan for actuating these ideas the next time you attend a funeral viewing, or seek to console someone who grieves. Keep your plan simple. Think through the way you will approach the situation the next time it arises so that you will be prepared and not have to wing it.

A blessing prayer for you:

Father, may our words be inspired and empowered by Your Holy Spirit. May we be agents of comfort and healing in the world around us.

Fifteen

KEY TO THE MINT: LEADERSHIP

Problem:

I am not a leader. I'm not the type of person who can make a difference in others.

Solution:

I hope that I am in the process of inspiring you to greater things. Part of this process is to help you see the leadership potential we all have. As we walk along beside those who are struggling, we are effecting leadership principles that help others navigate their unique crisis. So, to that end, I thought it would be valuable to share a huge lesson I learned from my dad... after he was gone.

Dad was a simple, hard-working, dedicated family man. He was a mighty man of God who never felt like He had done enough. He had a servant heart, and was broken for others. Yet dad struggled with the misplaced idea that he had missed his God-calling and had never done enough to make a difference in the lives of others.

When he died of cancer in his early 70s, there was a two and a half hour wait during the visitation. The next day, the church where we held the funeral was packed. Over and over I saw living testimonies of how my dad DID make a difference in the Name of Jesus.

I had the honor of delivering his eulogy. In the moments leading up to my words, a stark realization came over me as I scanned the crowd there to honor the life of Richard Fish. I had spent years studying many great leadership books, and that was good, but the greatest model of a leader stood right before me. My dad taught me, in very practical ways, what it means to be a leader in everyday life even if you don't consider yourself to be leadership material.

I began to distill the factors I found at work, and concluded there were five principles present that allowed dad to be a leader doing the simple, everyday things of life. The genius of these concepts is they are things we all can do.

These simple leadership principles form a healing, cohesive life ethic that will helps us to live effectively among people who hurt.

Here are the five principles of leadership in simple terms.

1. Take Them Fishing

My dad was an avid fisherman. In his last years, he had bought a boat and regularly took people fishing. At his funeral I heard countless stories about these forays. Interestingly enough, people tended not to talk about the catch that day, nor about how dad probably amazed them with his fish cleaning skills, but rather they spoke of the great conversations they had.

Dad built relationships. At the heart of the Gospel is the call to love others, to be a good neighbor, to take care of the needs around us. When we take time to build relationships, we begin to establish connections that open the doors of trust and good will.

Fishing is a metaphor for finding ways to come together socially with others in non-confrontational situations. Do things with others that have no other motive than to get to know them better and to do something loving for them. Maybe fishing is your thing. Maybe it's something else. Find ways to easily connect with others by using the social gifts you already have in place.

Taking them fishing means spending time, loving, giving of yourself, and building hope-inducing relationships.

2. Do One Right Thing After Another

Don't get bogged down with all the details about how to save the world. Don't let life's many options overwhelm you. Rather than letting the myriad of options overwhelm you, pick one and do it.

Dad may not have accomplished all that he wanted to do, but that didn't stop him from doing something. Every day he was busy doing one right thing after another. Even in this last months, as his strength left him, he was still plotting ways to be a help. This ethic was so ingrained in him that it stubbornly would not let him live any other way.

You're not going to be able to do every good thing that needs to be done. Pick one, and do it. Don't get frustrated with what is left undone. Don't get discouraged wondering which choice is more right than another. If it's right, do it. Once you get that done, pick another right thing and do it. This is a much surer route to accomplishing much and staying motivated.

Writing this book came from very similar advice. Do you know what the number one secret to writing a book is? It's to just do it. That made perfect sense to me, and today you hold the fruit of that counsel. In the same way, the key to accomplishing good things is to do them. Stop delaying, stop making excuses, and do good things. Do one right after the other.

3. Care Deeply

My dad loved people, and they knew it. Dad would take time for others even at the sacrifice of his own need at the moment. He was generous and concerned.

I suspect this is the type of quality most believers aspire to, but have the general sense that this gifting has alluded them. We WANT to care deeply, but there are so many distractions.

Dad's ability to care was genuinely born out of a daily, rich walk with Jesus. We take on the personality of those we hang out with, right?! Dad hung out with Jesus. He talked to Him often, thought about His Word often, and tried to take in opportunities to grow. If you are lacking in the care department, I would encourage you forward. Draw deeply into Christ and know that He is near. Get to know His ways, His beauty.

4. Say It

Put your love into words. Encourage. Tell people what you think they're doing well. Be lavish with positive, affirming words.

Dad struggled with a critical nature, just as I have. He knew that he was not always as helpfully affirming as his heart wanted to be. So he developed this trait of generously pouring out words of praise and affirmation. Though it was hard for dad to put his words into writing, he graciously left behind a few priceless letters to me where he built me up and expressed confidence and pride in me.

Others have told me about the difference dad's words of encouragement made to them. Be generous and liberal with your love words to others.

5. Create Family

Dad had the gift of bringing others into the family. If you knew dad, you had a brother, a father, a grandpa in him.

We typically offer our family a higher degree of regard than we do our friends, acquaintances, and others. I would encourage you to find ways to make others feel like family, to make them welcome. Perfect hospitality. Let them be more than friends; let them be at home with you.

These are all principles that are within the grasp of each one of us. These are things we all can do. These are things that make a difference and create leadership. Where these are present, others will look to you as a person worthy of respect and consideration. I can't tell you for sure how important it is to do all these things rather than picking one from the list and going for it. I can only reveal that I found these all in place in my dad, and came to the realization that they were part of how he changed the world.

Who are some of the people in your world that influenced you most? Try to distill similar principles from their life that you can apply to your own.

1. Challenge yourself to write down one good thing you'd like to accomplish, then post it where you'll see it often. Make this your first challenge and commit to do it.

2. Name at least three people that you know who seem to have the gift of caring deeply for others. How does this gift manifest itself? What are the qualities of these people that you would like to emulate in your own life?

3. Spend some time with the five points of everyday leadership mentioned in this chapter, praying over each one, and allow God to shine the light of revelation into your heart for how you can begin to do these things today.

A blessing prayer for you:

Father, may your mighty and bold strength so be a part of our daily routine that the world we walk through will be impacted by your glory even in our own weak, feeble steps.

Sixteen

KEY TO THE MINT: LIVING BEYOND REGRET

Problem:

I have so many regrets from mistakes I've made with people I've loved. Is it possible to live beyond regret?

Solution:

The concept of living beyond regret is rather pie-in-the-sky; it sounds great but isn't absolutely within reach.

What is the best we can do, then? How can I have the most amount of peace once the days I spend walking with someone who struggles have ended?

As a pastor, I've taken note of so many relationship nightmares that I determined I was going to learn my lesson and do all the right things to waylay regret. I was firmly resolute that I would live daily in such a way that when my loved ones were gone, I would know that all was well.

My wife's passing afforded me a profound opportunity to accomplish this since her bad health gave me years of warning that our time together would be shortened. Also, there were the many days she lingered and was responsive, giving me more opportunity to communicate my heart to her. But as the days after her death turned into weeks, and the weeks turned into months, I found that there were so many things I wanted to go back and say – so many do-overs I wish I had.

Keep in mind that the suggestions I'm about to give come with the qualifier that there is no perfect path to regret-free living, just some solid things we can do to promote peace of mind long into the future. Even though regret comes at me like a hungry lion, and my grieving heart looks like a big ol' pork chop to that lion, I find that the right things I did in advance are the chair and whip I need to fight off its advances.

I practice what I've come to know as a deep breath, holy pause method to bring me back to the reality that I really did do well in living out sound principles that helped me to say goodbye to the ones I didn't want to lose here in this life. So often it is best to stop, take a deep breath, know that He is God and allow Him to fill that moment of holy pause with His holy presence.

Here, then are some practical things you can do to ward off future regret:

1. Talk honestly.

Recognize that life is frail. Share your feelings and fears about loss. Find a way to communicate about the what-ifs of life.

This is particularly hard to do because we so easily dismiss conversations about death and dying. I think this is a big mistake. Because I was able to have many conversations with Barbara about how her illness might progress, we were able to formulate game plans, and I was able to learn more of her wishes. Best of all, she was able to console me in advance. It has been phenomenally helpful to retroactively hear her words of comfort ringing in my head and heart. I know that she didn't want to leave me, and that leaving me behind was as hard for her as losing her was for me.

This idea will be very difficult for many of you. Let me encourage you towards your own deep breath / holy pause moments so that you can have fulfilling, meaningful conversation that will serve you well once your loved one is gone.

2. Love lavishly.

This is particularly difficult for those of us who think one single "I love you" should suffice for a lifetime! Take every opportunity to express love in words, actions and body language.

3. Touch often.

Frankly, there are not enough words. I have thousands of words I still want to say to Barbara now that she's gone. I've walked along beside people who've lost loved ones suddenly, and they grieve over things unsaid. I've walked along beside people who had long goodbyes like mine, and they grieve over things unsaid. We can never say enough (even though that doesn't mean we shouldn't have meaningful conversations like I suggest in items 1 and 2.)

You will miss their touch someday, so touch them often. Hold hands if it's that kind of relationship. Touch shoulders. Hug, for crying out loud. Sit close. Don't be afraid of the silences. Touch often; those touches linger in helpful ways.

4. Bless them.

I can't understate the importance of spiritual encounters with the ones you love. Pray with them, for them, around them. Share faith-driven events and opportunities with them. Every day, I say it again, every day, speak blessings over them and into their life. Will the good of God into their day through your words. Encourage them with Psalms and songs.

5. Do good things with them just for the sake of doing good.

Don't underestimate the value of conspiring with your loved ones to do secret acts of kindness for others; these will be memories that will inspire you long after they're gone. These are ways of living the Good News of Christ that prepare us well for hard days.

—⟋ɷ⟍—

Begin a plan to live beyond regret by praying a blessing over your family. Simply put a hand on their shoulder and pray one good thing into their life.

1. Read through this chapter with someone you love and use it as a springboard to have conversation that will be the beginning of regret-ending discussions to come.

2. Experience tells me that there will be readers who find these ideas to be things they simply don't want to do, or don't believe they have the strength to do. If you find the objective of this chapter to be something you'd like to achieve - living beyond regret as best you can - spend time in prayer now asking the Holy Spirit to empower you to activate these ideas, or to discover your own workable ideas.

A blessing prayer for you:

May the Lord give you peace, good communication, and beautiful memories in all your vital relationships.

FINAL THINGS

Seventeen

BE PATIENT.
TAKE COURAGE.
DON'T GRUMBLE.

Jase worked for me for a few years in broadcasting. He had the perfect radio voice, boyish good looks, and enjoyed an endless assortment of dangerous hobbies. He was the sort of fellow that you just knew could do anything he wanted to do in life. And one of the things he really wanted to do was go spelunking.

Spelunking is cave diving. I might also be tempted to classify it as a mental illness, but that's just my take on it. Jase would regale me of stories of having to hold his breath for minutes while squeezing his body through a cave opening that might or might not be big enough for even someone as trim as he was to pass through. I would have called that a nightmare, but he called it fun. The thought of willingly trying to squeeze my claustrophobic frame through a dark, tiny expanse of an underground cave brings chills of horror to my system.

While writing this book I took a few diversions to clear my head. One such diversion was to visit a public cave in the area where I was camping for the writing process. I had been to other public caves before and found that they did not trigger any form of claustrophobia in me - even when they did the obligatory trick of turning out all the lights so you could see how dark darkness really is.

It didn't take me long to figure out that this tourist attraction was not the typical cave. It was a bit more rustic than others I'd been in. Much to my horror, it contained a few passages that were tight squeezes. Fortunately, they were very short passages, well lit, and quite spacious, I'm sure, compared to what hardcore spelunkers hope to encounter. I summoned my courage and pressed on. Obviously, I did not meet my demise hundreds of feet below ground level.

Interestingly enough, we were instructed not to touch anything in the cave. Hands off. And then we were invited to pass between these narrow passageways. But don't touch anything. Seriously.

I don't mean this to be a confession admissible in a court in case I broke any applicable laws, but I touched the cave. In fact, observing others, we all touched it.

Touching the cave leaves behind oils that, over time, deteriorate the cave. At the very start of the tour they pointed out a stalagmite (the kind of cave formation that moves from the ground up) that many people had handled over the years. It was one of the most sad, ugly, depressed stalagmites I'd ever seen. If you touch it, you change it.

Touch it, change it

By following Jesus to the side of those who hurt, we choose to touch a life in the hopes of changing their situation for the better. You may never experience any earthly reward, but your touch has surely made a difference. Your time, your care, your efforts have not been wasted. The willingness to make the way better for the struggling, suffering, hurting one can be a thankless journey at times, but for those who want to be where Jesus is, it's the exact place we'll find ourselves time and again.

Choosing to walk beside those in need allows us the privilege of also sharing their pain. I've learned that even though we don't share in the exact nature of the struggle, we share it nonetheless. Being made one through marriage with a woman who dealt with debilitating illness allowed me to understand this type of sympathetic pain in a personal way. Though most of the sharing comes in the form of the emotional, your body will also react physically at times to the struggle as well. So, as we touch a life and change it, we are also experiencing the change as well. It's a refining process that God uses to make us better, and more fit for what is to come. In scripture, James describes it this way:

> *Dear brothers and sisters, when troubles come your way, consider it an opportunity for great joy. For you know that when your faith is tested, your endurance has a chance to grow. So let it grow, for when your endurance is fully developed, you will be perfect and complete, needing nothing.* *James 1:2-4 (NLT)*

I resonate with this words. I get it. One exercise I enjoy to help me process scripture is to write it out in my own words. It creates a journal of my journey in the Word. Here is how I processed this passage:

> *The very fact that we are given the opportunity and the smarts to adapt and grow should be great news... so much so that we are the people known for JOY! Let your faith grow... don't stifle it... because it will grow into being everything you need!*

Later, in chapter 5 of James, we get some instruction that has remained on my wall wherever I've worked to remind me of a vital life principle. As you will notice, I have edited the passage. A bunch. Please read it all on your own later, but for now, here is a stark, eye-opening rendering of some verses that will be very formative as you move forward with the ideas expressed in this book:

Be patient.
Take courage.
Don't grumble.
James 5:7-8 (edited)

Write those words down in a place where you'll see them often. Let them shape you. Let them encourage you. Let them challenge you. Let them expose things in you that need to be addressed.

The difficulties you encounter as you do the difficult work of this book are your seeds of growth.

How Not to Kill Someone

I used to occasionally watch one of those shows chronicling encounters with hoarders. After watching one of those shows I always felt like I needed to take a shower, clean house whether it needed it or not, then get rid of as much stuff as I could.

One episode featured an animal hoarder, and this man's attraction was of the feline variety. Think with me, if you will, about what happens in a house brimming with cats. If you've ever tried to manage the filth of just a few indoor pets, imagine that multiplied by unreasonable amounts. A home in this state is not fit for man nor beast. The end result was a sick old man and hundreds of kitties in varying states of bad health.

As they showed the man a few of the dead cats, he began to cry, "I wondered what had happened to Fluffy!"

His excuse was simple. He believed he was saving the cats. They needed somewhere to go, so he took them in. He thought he was being compassionate. Instead, he was killing the very creatures he intended to rescue.

As a pastor, I've seen plenty of churches where this same principle was in place. Instead of saving people, they were killing them. Really, this can happen in any kind of community of people. Good intentions are not enough, we must be empowered by something greater, something that produces sound principles.

This is precisely why I wanted to end with the reminder to be patient, take courage, and don't grumble. The very one you're trying to help needs this of you. If you truly want to help, than I encourage you not to kill them (even in, of course, the most metaphorical of ways). Their salvation, if you will, will be aided by your patience, courage, and refusal to grumble.

I'll break this down with some final pieces of great encouragement for how to move forward from here:

1. Don't worry about getting everything right at first.

This one can really trip us up.

When I a program director at a radio station, I would hire young folks who expected that they would be perfected as an on-air personality the moment they opened the mic. Surely, they thought, everyone would love to hear them drone on endlessly and find it to be compelling. You've no doubt seen similar examples where you work.

Experience is the growth engine. Like James 1 reminds us, trouble (or testing, or trials) are opportunity for joy because they teach us to be better. In the meantime, don't despise the days of learning.

OK, sure, I still kick myself over things I did in the early days of my life with Barbara. I think of the times that I was not properly sensitive to her pain. I had to learn to be the man she needed me to be (this applies in so many ways beyond the scope of this book!). In the end, she never once reminded me of the mistakes I'd made. I suspect that she was also haunted by things she wished she'd done differently. Instead, she continually assured me that I was a good husband and a good man. I was never perfect, but I did well because I grew.

Allow yourself the privilege and honor of growth, because you'll need. It. Be patient. Take courage. Don't grumble.

2. Get out of the zone of clarity.

Your faith in God will serve you well in serving others. Faith says that we believe in something beyond what we can see. We may not have perfect clarity in all things relating to God, but we have faith that fills in the gaps. As you are in the role of walking beside others, there will be little clarity. When will this end? Will it end? How will it end? What will tomorrow bring? Will things get better or worse? These questions are issues of clarity that living in a moment cannot bring. On the other hand, faith tells us there is more, there is something better.

Certainty causes us to look at what we have in hand and decide we can't make it based on what we see. We need to get out of that zone.

Faith causes us to submit to a Savior, One who is able to do what we cannot do for ourselves.

And remember this, too. Grumbling happens because we observe what we have in the zone of clarity. When we look at our present affliction, grumbling is the natural result. Who wouldn't grumble if they had to deal with what we have to face here in the zone of clarity? Grumbling, though, is not a faith response. We grumble because we lack faith.

Courage, on the other hand, causes us to move ahead despite what we have in hand at the moment. Faith inspires courage because we learn to see that there is so much more ahead.

Be patient. Take courage. Don't grumble.

3. Remember God's power.

If James is right, faith brings wisdom and joy. And if we subscribe to that line of thinking, what does that mean many of us lack?

If James is right, and I think he is, then faith will produce the ability to not only see our way clearly through the situations that prevail, but to also do it with joy. Knowledge must be learned, but wisdom can come in an instant. Wisdom is the way we parse what we know, or what we can gather. Joy is an overwhelming sense of well-being even when in the company of great distress.

How, then, do we live in the kind of faith that produces wisdom and joy when we can barely make sense of the moment we face at present? Remember God's power. He can do what you and I cannot do. He is able, we are weak.

As I've spoken of walking beside the one who suffers, I've often paired it with the reminder that we follow Jesus to that place. Not everyone intends to follow Him there, but when we do compassionate work like that, He is there. It's good that we remind ourselves that when it comes to the suffering of this world, God's plan was for His believers to go to the aid of those who hurt. We are God's plan A, plan B, and so forth. We are in a fallen world that hurts. Hurting is not a sign of God's powerlessness, it's a call for us to receive God's holy presence and move in His power. This is the only way we can do the hard work of helping others with any real semblance of hope.

You cannot do this. I cannot do this. But in Christ, we can. He is our power. The very same power that rose Jesus from the dead is the power available to us today. It is the power that gives us the ability to be patient, to take courage, and to avoid grumbling.

So what will we take hold of, then?

Remember the story I told of Mrs. Richardson, the teacher who told me in rather strong words that if I didn't stop with the negative attitude, my life would be "One bad thing after another"? Remember how I told you she drove the point home by pounding her fist on the table in rhythm with the words?

I want you to hear that again and make up your mind today that you will move forward with great faith that God is doing great things in you and through you. You don't need to be concerned about reward or recognition, for you're on a much greater mission.

The other option is to let negativity overwhelm us and live a life that is one bad thing after another. Pound, pound, p-pound.

Our powerful God invites us to come with him into the hard things, the uneasy places. In doing so we have great grace and power availed to us. Be patient, I say again. Take courage, I repeat. Don't grumble, I say in as non-grumbly a manner as I can.

To do otherwise is to labor in the land of defeat where there is one bad thing after another, one bad day after another.

We can do this because we love the One who makes us able. Now go and serve well.

—⟋ℳ⟍—

Look up and read James chapters 1 and 5. Then, write out the words, "Take courage, Be patient, Don't grumble" and place them where you'll see them often.

1. Can you reflect on, and identify, hurtful and painful things that happened in your life that ended up making you stronger? What do you think James meant when he said our struggles will produce endurance that makes us complete?

2. We're in a time where the topic of bullies is discussed quite a bit. Do you think we consider enough how easily we all can become bullies when we live a grumbling, discouraging, courage-less lifestyle? How do the lack of these three principles cause us to "kill" others?

3. How has this chapter helped you to better adjust the expectations you put on yourself for getting everything right all at once?

4. Why is the "zone of clarity" not such a good place for the faithful believer to live after all?

5. Do you think believers today are more aware or less aware of the power available to us through God? What things need to take place to help us better teach others the power of living through faith? How can this impact the way we come along beside those who hurt?

A blessing prayer for you:

May the power of the Father in Heaven be yours, may it produce many good things as you walk with Him and at the side of others. May great confidence be given to you by the steadfast presence of our Father in Heaven.

Epilogue

THE FIRST CHRISTMAS
AND OTHER ENDINGS

In the back of my garage is a place where Christmas decorations are safely tucked away. Plastic containers, seemingly as many as there are birds in the sky, loaded full of now sacred snowmen and ornaments and other holiday niceties are stacked one on top of the other. And there I stood, in the late November cold, hesitant to advance towards them.

Thanksgiving had passed, and now, Christmas seemed inevitable.

I took a deep breath and mumbled to myself something about this being the first Christmas, and proceeded to the heart-wrenching task of opening containers to see what I might want to use this year, this inaugural season of my new life.

Through a curtain of tears I struggled vainly to find the Peanut characters that I loved and Barbara tolerated. OK, so I think she loved them too because she knew I enjoyed Charlie Brown and the gang, all frozen in time from my all time favorite Christmas special. But they were hopelessly buried beneath a barrier of memories.

Barbara didn't want jewelry. She didn't want me to spend our money buying her cut flowers. What she loved was home decorations. She could spend hours searching the right stores for just the right treasure to hang on a wall or place on a shelf. Most of the time she would end up insisting that she didn't really need it. But, when I could tell her heart had been captured, it was my pleasure to encourage the purchase. She treasured these things, and I helped her to arrange them with the finest precision. Over the years it became a joke that anything on a shelf had to be perfectly off-center and artfully placed at an right angle. I would muster my best HGTV interior designer impression as I dutifully served as her arms and legs in the task of making our house a home.

That is why it became impossible for me to sort through the myriad of Christmas trimmings. They were too intimately connected to her for me to be able to handle them that first Christmas. So, wanting something Christmasy without the major labor that decking of the halls usually entailed, I settled on just the tree.

This was a special skinny tree standing about four or five feet tall that was the just right for the two of us. It was quite pretty and fashionable with its realistic branches and tiny rice lights that twinkled and glittered. Such beauty came at a cost, though. The needles are wiry and sharp, and my hand felt like it was being attacked by hundreds of stinging bumble bees every time I reached inside to grab the tree at its center to move it.

We kept the tree in a large, sturdy plastic bag, and we would pack it away fully decorated. I had forgotten that after her last Christmas here, she had wanted to do something different with the tree next year. Next year had arrived, and the tree was empty except for lights and the occasional attached small pinecone. But that seemed about right. It was beautiful and empty all at the same time.

As I sat on the couch wistfully trying to enjoy the lighted tree, I was surprised to make a discovery. One lone heart ornament remained clinging to the lower branches. Just one heart had escaped notice and remained there for me to find. Perhaps it was divine, perhaps not. I moved the heart to a prominent place on the tree, and reminded myself that it was well with my soul.

My mind fades back to the early days of my relationship with Barbara. We would sit close together there in that pew at the Free Methodist Church in Columbus, Indiana, and draw hearts on the back of each other's hands with our fingers as a way to say, "I love you," when it would not have otherwise been appropriate to say out loud.

Still today the Father finds way to etch his love into my heart, quietly, softly, faithfully.

Endings

I have spent this this time with you talking about things that are important to remember when we walk beside those who suffer. My Christmas decorating experience reminded me that there was one final thing to say. Sometimes it ends.

When we care deeply for the needs of others, endings can be extraordinarily painful. We call that grief. When we follow Christ to the side of the hurting, when we accept his commission to love, there will be a great sense of loss when that walk comes to an end, whether it's family, friend, or just a passing acquaintance.

Years ago, a pastor gave me what proved to be both the best and worst advice for ministry. He told me to never get close to people, to never let myself get personally involved. It would only hurt me. I believe that the things I measure as my greatest successes in ministry have come because I did allow myself to love people deeply, and to care about them as more than just parishioners. I admit, though, that he was right on the hurting part. Giving myself freely to love and serve others has brought great depths of hurting at times. Still, I have never regretted the love.

Love, hanging there like a lone heart ornament on a Christmas tree, reminds us that even in the pain of endings and goodbye, we know we did the right thing. Anything it cost, anything it took away, we can count as gain.

Many Christmases ago, my nieces were coloring while at my house. The youngest, Carly, handed me the white crayon and informed me that it was "broke."

I looked at it, confused by what she meant since it was clearly still in one piece. My sister solved the mystery by telling me that since the crayon was white, and Carly couldn't see the color when she used it, she assumed the crayon was... broke.

And so it is that we may still be in one piece without one visible scratch or scar, and yet feel as though we are... broke. These are the moments where once again we take a deep breath, a holy pause, and allow healing to ready us for whatever lies ahead.

Do good things. Follow Jesus to the side of those who hurt. Love freely and without condition. And when the end comes, cry and grieve and know that all is well with your soul. Celebrate the treasure of the journey, and use it to grow stronger for the road ahead. Then, when you sense that Christ is slowing you down once again, look around and take note of the need waiting to be met. Meet the need. Serve well. Keep moving towards home. And in the quiet moments, listen carefully and you might just here Jesus gently reminding you with soft words, "I will walk with you."

Printed in the United States
By Bookmasters